Man and Battle
Carrier Victory: The Air War in the Pacific

CARRIER VICTORY:

A Talisman / Parrish Book

THE AIR WAR
IN THE PACIFIC

John M. Lindley

Elsevier-Dutton
New York

COPY 8

ISBN: 0-525-93002-7

Published in the United States by E. P. Dutton,
a Division of Sequoia-Elsevier Publishing Company, Inc., New York
Published simultaneously in Canada by
Clarke, Irwin & Company Limited, Toronto and Vancouver

Art Direction: The Etheredges
Production Manager: Stephen Konopka

Printed in the U.S.A.   First Edition
10 9 8 7 6 5 4 3 2 1

Contents

Preface

This is a book about life on an aircraft carrier in World War II. As much as possible the narrative uses the words and thoughts of men, seamen to admirals, who served aboard the flattops of the United States, Japanese and British navies rather than accounts by third persons who might not have been there.

Although the Royal Navy contributed significantly to the development of the aircraft carrier prior to 1939, and it had a substantial carrier force throughout the war, its European foes operated navies which were essentially without carriers. Hence this narrative concerns almost exclusively the war in the Pacific, where the principal carrier-versus-carrier sea-air battles took place. There is no "typical" example of life on a carrier during World War II, because of the multiplicity and complexity of operations over vast areas of the Pacific. In addition, there was no one solution to the problems which commanders in the three carrier navies faced. For example, U.S. carriers had to be "long-legged" in their logistic capacities because they had to operate far from their bases of supply. The Japanese and British carriers, in contrast, were basically "short-legged"; they operated much closer to their bases and did not have the capacity for under-way replenishment of fuel oil, food, ammunition and aviation gasoline comparable to those of the Americans.

The operation of aircraft carriers as ships of war is only half of the carrier story. These capital ships would have been exceedingly vulnerable without their "main battery" of aircraft. Thus this narrative gives equal weight to the accounts of the men who flew from the carriers taking war to the enemy, whether at sea or ashore. The story of the men who man the carriers and that of those who flew the planes carried by these ships combine to make a single story.

In writing this account of life on aircraft carriers of the navies of the United States, Japan and Great Britain, I have received helpful suggestions and ideas from a great number of persons. In particular, the staffs of the St. Olaf College Library, the Carleton College Library, the Northfield, Minnesota, Public Library and the St. Paul Public Library were most willing to search out material that I needed. Mr. James Earl Crow, a veteran SBD radioman/tail gunner, helped correct my misunderstandings of air operations in the war and kept me going with a nearly endless flow of stories about life on a carrier. I also thank Mr. Lee M. Pearson, retired historian, Naval Air Systems Command, for encouraging my interest in the history of aviation and carrier operations. And I particularly urge the reader to make use of the section of the book entitled "For Further Reading," where he will find the principal sources that I have drawn upon and will likewise find himself or herself directed to a great deal of enlightening and fascinating reading.

Finally, I am indebted to the insight and perception of my wife, Susan, who understood why I wanted to write this book.

JOHN M. LINDLEY

1. **Pearl Harbor**

When Commander Mitsuo Fuchida of the Imperial Japanese Navy signaled
TO . . . TO . . . TO in Morse code from his plane to his superiors aboard
the command ship of the Pearl Harbor Striking Force, the pilots in this
first wave were ready for the attack—and they were amazed at the absence
of enemy antiaircraft defense. The "TO" signal literally meant "charge," and
it told Vice Admiral Chuichi Nagumo and his staff for the Hawaiian Operation, as it was officially designated, that their planes were attacking the
U.S. fleet at Pearl Harbor. Four minutes later, at 7:53 A.M., on Sunday,
7 December, 1941, Fuchida's radioman tapped out the second key signal:
TORA . . . TORA . . . TORA. TORA was the code word "tiger," which carried the message "We have succeeded in surprise attack."

Chief Flight Petty Officer Juzo Mori was one of those torpedo bomber
pilots who dived on one of the enemy battleships that Sunday morning. He
thought there would be heavy antiaircraft fire, and he did not expect to
survive the attack. Consequently he set his mind on getting a battleship,
even if it cost him his life. Since the initial waves of Japanese planes had
aroused defensive fire from the Americans, he had to fly directly through

1

Pearl Harbor: the battle fleet lies waiting

it. Nevertheless, the antiaircraft fire did not seem to affect his aircraft's performance.

Mori swung his torpedo bomber into position for an approach on a battleship. As he said later, he knew the approach had to be "absolutely correct" because of the shallow depth of the Pearl Harbor channel. A faulty approach would cause his torpedo to bury its nose in the channel bottom or to jump from the surface, destroying its aim.

Once he began his attack, Mori "was hardly conscious" of what he was doing. As his plane dived toward his target, he sensed that he was "reacting from habit instilled by long training, moving like an automaton." He reached 2,000 feet. "Suddenly the battleship appeared to have leaped forward directly in front of my speeding plane," Mori said later. "It towered ahead of the bomber like a great mountain peak." He concentrated with a single mind on his mission: "Prepare for release . . . Stand by! Release torpedo!"

Oblivious of the defensive fire of the American warships, Mori pulled the release lever with all the force he could muster, at just the right moment. As the torpedo broke free of its bonds, the aircraft pitched and bucked from the antiaircraft fire. Mori's head snapped back and he "felt as though a heavy beam had struck" it.

With his torpedo gone on what he judged was a perfect attack, Chief Petty Officer Mori realized that enemy fire was now smashing into his plane. He headed the bomber due south toward the sea and made good his escape. "I was so frightened," Mori recalled, "that before I left the target area my clothes were soaking with perspiration."

Some Japanese pilots were not as fortunate as Mori. Lieutenant Fusata Iida was a squadron leader of a group of Zero fighters which attacked the U.S. Naval Air Station at Kaneohe. Iida and his men quickly destroyed a handful of American fighters defending the field and then closed to strafe it. During this strafing run, antiaircraft fire hit Iida's plane, which began to spray gasoline. According to Lieutenant (jg) Iyozo Fujita, who was also there, Iida's Zero suddenly "whipped over into an inverted position and dove vertically for the enemy positions below." Fujita thought Iida was just making another run on the field until he realized the plane was flying in a most unusual manner, "as it dove in its vertical, inverted position until it exploded on the ground between the Kaneohe airfield hangars."

On the ground, all was confusion initially. The American soldiers and sailors were caught so completely by surprise that their first reactions were too late to deter the attackers. But once the military personnel realized that this was for real, that this was no Army or Navy trick maneuver, the hours spent in training for war began to assert themselves. About four minutes after the first bombs began to fall, Rear Admiral Patrick N. L. Bellinger, who commanded the naval aviation forces on Oahu, broadcast:

AIR RAID, PEARL HARBOR—THIS IS NO DRILL.

Other messages, alerting U.S. forces elsewhere of the attack, went out in a hurry.

On Battleship Row were moored seven dreadnoughts—*Maryland, Oklahoma, Tennessee, West Virginia, Arizona, California* and *Nevada.* Another battlewagon, *Pennsylvania,* was in drydock across the harbor. Five cruisers and 26 destroyers and minecraft were also tied up in various places around the harbor.

Those crew members who were aboard these warships that Sunday morning did what they could to fight back. Since many senior officers and chief petty officers were on shore leave for the weekend, the task of leading the defensive fire sometimes fell on very junior and inexperienced shoulders. Ensign J. K. Taussig, officer of the deck on *Nevada,* ordered his ship-

Arizona blazes furiously following an explosion

mates to Battle Stations, had the ship's hatches, ports and other outside openings closed up, and passed the word over the PA system: "All hands, general quarters. Air raid! This is no drill!"

Because Taussig had ordered the engine room to bring a second boiler on line during the earlier portion of his watch, *Nevada* had the minimum of two boilers needed to get under way without the four tugs normally used. While the ship's machine guns and portside 5-inch batteries tried to ward off the attacking Japanese, Chief Quartermaster Robert Sedberry skillfully backed the battleship down, then went astern on his port engines and

Fireboat pours water onto the burning *West Virginia*

ahead on the starboard screws to twist the ship's bow clear of *Arizona*, burning nearby. He then went ahead on both engines deftly using right rudder to swing the stern clear and out into the channel.

When Harbor Control realized that *Nevada* was under way, they feared that the attackers might sink her in the middle of the channel. They therefore signaled the battlewagon to stay clear of the main passage. Taussig, who by this time was wounded in the left leg, was angry with this order, but the senior officer aboard followed it and *Nevada* was beached on Hospital Point just as three bombs landed near the bow, killing everyone who was nearby.

No other ship was lucky enough to escape. *California* took two torpedo hits and a bomb, which set off a magazine. *Arizona* suffered both bomb and torpedo hits, which tore the ship apart. One of her forward magazines exploded, trapping hundreds of men below decks. Despite the damage, she fought back until about 10:30, when the order was given to abandon ship. Nevertheless, *Arizona* suffered 1,103 officers and men killed out of a total of 1,400 on board.

Oklahoma suffered heavily too. She took three torpedo hits and was abandoned in the early minutes of the attack. By 8:15 she lay bottom up. Many of those who left *Oklahoma* climbed aboard the nearby *Maryland* and kept up the fight. This battleship was protected from the attackers by her sunken counterpart and took only two bomb hits and no torpedoes.

West Virginia was less fortunate. She took at least six torpedo hits and two bombs. Yet her spirited crew somehow fought the fires, counter-flooded to control the damage below decks, and kept firing at the enemy planes. *Tennessee*, which was inboard of *West Virginia*, took two bomb hits and had some fires, but generally suffered much less than her sister battle-wagons.

Pennsylvania, flagship of the Pacific Fleet, put up a sturdy defense from her position in the drydock. Since the drydock protected her from the torpedoes, she struck back at the enemy with all the antiaircraft fire she could muster. Unfortunately, the U.S. Navy's machine guns were not very effective. The smaller caliber 1.1-inch tended to overheat and jam, while the 3-inch was not rapid firing enough. *Pennsylvania* took one severe bomb hit and lost 18 men killed. Several bombs meant for the flagship hit the nearby destroyers *Cassin* and *Downes*, which were also in the Navy dry-dock.

At 8:55 A.M. a second wave of Japanese attackers hit Pearl Harbor. Although smaller in number than the first, the second attack group nevertheless had plenty of punch with 36 fighters, 54 high-level bombers and 80 dive-bombers. This force immediately struck at *Pennsylvania* and *Nevada*, which were putting up determined defensive fire.

7

By this time the Japanese planes were not the only ones in the air over the harbor area. A dozen Army B-17s had left the mainland 14 hours earlier for Hawaii. Reaching their destination between 8:00 and 9:00 that morning, the big bombers were powerless to do anything about the attack. They had been stripped down before leaving—they carried no armor and no ammunition, and their guns were packed in cosmoline. Some of the bombers managed to land safely, only to be destroyed once on the ground. Others survived unscathed.

In addition to the B-17s, Army pilots were able to get a few fighter planes in the air before they were destroyed by bombs and strafing on the ground. These pilots managed to shoot down 11 attackers. Two of the pilots, Lieutenants Kenneth Taylor and George Welch, were responsible for downing seven Japanese planes.

When questioned after the war about the designated targets in the attack, Captain Yasuji Watanabe, a Japanese staff officer, responded that the "first aim was at aircraft carriers, but they were out at sea," so the Japanese attacked the other ships. The three carriers in the U.S. Pacific Fleet, *Saratoga*, *Lexington* and *Enterprise*, were not at Pearl Harbor on 7 December. *Saratoga* was en route to the mainland for repairs and upkeep. *Lexington* had departed Pearl Harbor on 5 December to deliver 25 planes to Midway Island. *Enterprise*, under Vice Admiral William F. Halsey, was returning to Pearl Harbor, having just delivered more Marine Corps fighters to Wake Island. Unlike most of the Americans in and around Hawaii in late 1941, Halsey had taken the warnings of possible war seriously and he had ordered his task force to be ready to shoot if it encountered hostile ships or aircraft.

At 6:15 on the morning of 7 December, the first SBD Dauntless dive-bombers in *Enterprise*'s scouting force were launched to search ahead of Halsey's task force. Most of those on board considered the dive-bomber aviators to be lucky, since they would probably arrive at Pearl a full six hours ahead of the ships. By 8:35 the leading SBDs were over the island and under fire from the Japanese. At first they thought the black puffs from antiaircraft fire were the result of an unusual Sunday target practice, but when the aviators saw what "looked like a lot of burning cigarette butts flash" from a plane with the red disk of the Rising Sun on wings and fuselage, the members of Scouting Six knew they were at war and under attack.

Some of the SBDs managed to shake off the Japanese and land in a hurry. Others were not so fortunate. Ensign Manuel Gonzales was never seen again, but his last words, "Please don't shoot! Don't shoot! This is an American plane," followed by an order to his rear-seatman "We're on fire,

8

Demolished B-17 sits on a taxiway at Hickam Field

bail out!" alerted *Enterprise* to the trouble ahead. Another ensign, John H. L. Vogt, was probably shot down by two or three Zeros in a dogfight.

Since the Dauntless was built for dive-bombing, it was no match for the fast, maneuverable Zero. Even so, Roger Miller, the rear-seat gunner in Lieutenant (jg) C. E. Dickinson's SBD, managed to shoot a Zero down before the bullets from other Zeros got him. Dickinson landed unhurt at Ewa Field. Other fliers had equally hazardous escapes from the attackers before landing.

When the communications watch aboard *Enterprise* picked up the transmissions from Ensign Gonzales and the others in Scouting Six, it immediately alerted Admiral Halsey to the situation at Pearl. The admiral signaled his force to prepare for battle and ordered planes in the air to search for the enemy and to provide combat air patrol (CAP) as a close-in defense around the task force.

All day long the *Enterprise* planes patrolled and searched for the Japanese fleet. A report of an enemy fleet to the south of Oahu drew a response from the carrier's strike force of Torpedo Six and Bombing Six, but instead of the Japanese they found only a number of friendly cruisers and destroyers that had fought their way out of Pearl and were trying to join up with Halsey. This meant that the carrier had to recover the planes, still armed with their bombs and torpedoes, after sunset.

When the *Enterprise* strike group had safely returned on board, its fighter escorts headed for Pearl because they lacked enough fuel to reach the ship. While approaching Ford Island after having received a landing clearance from the tower, the fighter pilots switched on their landing lights in preparation for touchdown. Suddenly a nervous gunner began firing at the planes. Then antiaircraft fire from all over the harbor converged on the fighters. Some pilots quickly extinguished their lights and escaped unharmed, but the trigger-happy defenders still managed to down four of the fighters before they ceased fire.

Because Admiral Halsey's scouts from *Enterprise* were unable to locate the Japanese fleet, no naval duel between ships or aircraft followed the attack on Pearl Harbor. The confusion on Oahu on 7 December and what seemed to be the disappearance of the Japanese forces after their mission was completed were indicative of the thoroughness with which their operation was planned and exercised.

No one was quite sure where the Japanese planes had come from. Undoubtedly an enemy carrier task force was in the area, but there were no quick answers to the questions of where it was and how large it was. Actually, the Pearl Harbor Striking Force, under the command of Vice Admiral Chuichi Nagumo, consisted of six of Japan's largest carriers and a screen to protect the carriers of nine destroyers and a light cruiser. These ships had a support force of two battleships and two heavy cruisers, and a supply train of seven or eight tankers. In addition, three submarines patrolled the force's flanks.

Japanese carrier *Hiryu,* part of the
Pearl Harbor Striking Force

From the very beginning of their planning, the Japanese had considered the carriers with their air arm as the main battery in the attack. The six carriers—*Akagi* (which meant Red Castle), *Kaga* (Increased Joy), *Soryu* (Green Dragon), *Hiryu* (Flying Dragon), *Shokaku* (Soaring Crane) and *Zuikaku* (Happy Crane)—carried a total of 423 combat planes. Of these they lost only 29, from all causes. Many of Japan's pilots and air crews had fought in the war that Japan had been waging with China since 1937. They were skilled veterans of aerial combat.

The plan for striking at Pearl Harbor had undergone a long and elaborate development. In the 1930s Japan's admirals formulated their strategic plans on the premise that, in a war with Japan, the American fleet would depart from Pearl Harbor and head west to strike the first blow. The Japanese, in turn, would harass the U.S. fleet with submarines, weaken it as it moved westward, and finally destroy it in their own waters, probably in the vicinity of Iwo Jima or Saipan. But Admiral Isoroku Yamamoto, Commander in Chief of the Japanese Combined Fleet, changed all that.

While observing the operations of Japan's carrier aircraft during training maneuvers in the spring of 1940, Yamamoto announced to his chief of staff, Rear Admiral Shigeru Fukudome: "I think an attack on Hawaii may be possible now that our air training has turned out so successfully." Yamamoto's statement was startling for two reasons. Less than a year earlier, he had publicly predicted that the United States would defeat Japan in any war between the two. Now he proposed to destroy the main forces of the

U.S. Navy in a single blow. The second surprise was that the admiral's plan turned upon a complete dependence on the fast carriers and their air weapons. In other words, carriers and their aircraft could do to the U.S. fleet what he had previously believed battleships and submarines could not do—make a Japanese victory possible.

In early 1941 Yamamoto set his staff to work making studies and plans for the attack. After studying the idea, the admiral's staff concluded that the attack would be difficult to mount and that it involved some risk, but that it contained "a reasonable chance of success." By April the plan had been named Operation Z and the Navy's aviation staff was hard at work refining the details of the operation and working out the techniques that would be needed. For example, a new torpedo was developed which could be used in the shallow channel at Pearl Harbor. By midsummer, carrier pilots were practicing their torpedo bombing techniques at Kagoshima Bay, which was similar in topography and layout to Pearl Harbor. By September 1941, Operation Z was in its final planning stages.

The plan for Operation Z had a logic that appealed to its originators. In 1904 the great Admiral Togo had attacked the Russian fleet at Port Arthur without a declaration of war and had dealt the Russians a blow from which they had never recovered. This plan for Pearl Harbor might also bring a decisive victory with one quick surprise attack.

Captain Yasuji Watanabe summed up the objective of the attack this way:

"In Japanese tactics we are told when we have two enemies, one in front and one in the back, first we must cut in front by [the] sword. Only cut and not kill, but make it hard. Then we attack the back enemy [presumably the British and Dutch forces in Asia] and kill him. Then we come back to the front enemy and kill him. This time we took that tactic, having no aim to capture Pearl Harbor but just to cripple it. We might have returned to capture [it] later."

Strike at Pearl Harbor to cripple the U.S. fleet. Then hit the British and Dutch to destroy their forces in Singapore, Hong Kong and the East Indies. Finally, return to destroy the Americans. All of this was based on two assumptions: first, that the U.S. fleet, particularly its carriers, would be at Pearl Harbor when the Japanese carrier planes attacked; and, second, that the Japanese striking force could cross the Pacific undetected and achieve complete surprise.

To maximize the possibility of achieving surprise, the Japanese naval planners chose a northerly route east across the Pacific. Although they knew that this route would plunge the Pearl Harbor force into winter

Admiral Yamamoto

storms, they judged that problems with the weather could be overcome with training. Because they had to avoid observation by American patrol planes, the naval staff chose their route with great care. They sent three submarines ahead to give warning of an approaching fleet, and they also decided to maintain complete radio silence prior to the attack.

By the end of November 1941 the Pearl Harbor Attack Force was trained and ready. It sortied from Hitokappu Bay, where the various ships had met in rendezvous on 2 December, with "X-Day" designated as 8 December (Tokyo time; 7 December in Hawaii). Admiral Nagumo's instructions were explicit on what to do in the event of discovery. If his force was observed more than two days prior to the attack, it was to return to Japan. If it was discovered the day before the attack or on the morning of 7 December, the force was to execute its orders to strike Hawaii regardless. If, of course, the negotiations which Japan was conducting with the U.S. government were successfully concluded, then the attack would be canceled. None of these contingency plans had to be used. The striking force proceeded to the area about 200 miles north of Oahu without incident, and it completely escaped detection that might have alerted the American forces in Hawaii.

Ironically, nearly everything went according to the Japanese plan except that the U.S. carriers, the primary objective, were all at sea. The attack did great damage to the U.S. fleet, as Admiral Yamamoto had hoped. As Captain Fuchida explained, "We knew we had done in four battleships, but [we] did not know the extent of damage to American planes, and of

13

course the carriers were not there. We figured if we could sink four battleships, then [the attack] was a success." Subsequently, the striking force withdrew to the west to avoid any counterattack. But the precious carriers—a factor more vital than anyone yet knew—had escaped. The Japanese had indeed inflicted heavy damage, but they had not won a strategic victory. The world was soon to see the proof.

2. Mobilization for War

The results of the Japanese attack on Pearl Harbor were exceedingly gratifying to Admiral Yamamoto and his staff. Prior to the strike on 7 December, the U.S. forces on Oahu had included nearly 400 aircraft and 7 battleships, but the raid had completely destroyed 188 Army and Navy planes and damaged another 31. Five battleships were now out of action, along with a number of other ships. The American forces had also lost 2,335 men killed and 1,143 personnel wounded. Japanese losses, in contrast, were minuscule: 29 aircraft and fewer than 100 men.

Around 6:00 P.M. on the day following the attack, *Enterprise* tied up at Pearl Harbor to resupply before heading out to sea to look for the Japanese. As the lines of sailors that made up the working parties bringing the supplies aboard the "Big E" moved box after box from pier to deck, word quickly passed that while he surveyed the widespread destruction in the harbor, Admiral Halsey had been heard to mutter, "Before we're through with 'em, the Japanese language will be spoken only in hell!"

By dawn the next day *Enterprise* was resupplied and at sea again. On 10 December Halsey spoke to his pilots about what had to be done. The

15

diary of Fighting Six, the ship's fighter squadron, summed up the admiral's message in one sentence: "Those Japs had better look out for that man." Halsey's pep talk apparently worked, because he got results that same day. *Enterprise* pilots spotted three surfaced enemy submarines during air patrols. Although one crash-dived and escaped, the other two were not so lucky. An SBD Dauntless from Bombing Six scored a direct hit on one sub as it tried to dive, and the third became the first combatant ship sunk by U.S. forces in World War II.

This submarine had chosen to fight it out with the *Enterprise* planes on the surface. Lieutenant Ed Anderson of Scouting Six dive-bombed and damaged it. Then Lieutenant Clarence Dickinson of the same squadron flew through the sub's antiaircraft fire to drop his bomb alongside amidships. The sub, *I-70,* stopped, went dead in the water, and then disappeared from sight, leaving only an expanding patch of oil and debris.

The sinking of *I-70* was not the only setback the Japanese suffered in early December. A small force of U.S. Navy and Marine forces stationed on Wake Island—lying between Oahu and Midway Island—had repulsed an attempted Japanese landing on 11 December. Consequently, Admiral Nagumo detached carriers *Soryu* and *Hiryu* (Carrier Division 2) from his retiring Pearl Harbor Strike Force to provide air support for the second landing attempt.

In the meantime, a U.S. Navy relief force commanded by Rear Admiral Frank Jack Fletcher was 500 miles east of the island. Fletcher had the carrier *Saratoga* and a number of destroyers to assist the men on Wake. Unfortunately, he never got close enough to provide any help. At first he had received orders to attack the Japanese force when he was within 200 miles of the Wake garrison, but that order, as well as an order to evacuate the personnel on Wake, was countermanded by Fletcher's superiors.

Although members of Admiral Fletcher's staff had recommended that he disobey his orders to withdraw, Fletcher refused. He was unsure whether those up the chain of command might be aware of greater dangers than he had knowledge of. Shortly thereafter the Americans on Wake surrendered and Tokyo Rose mockingly broadcast, "Where, oh where, is the United States Navy?"

Halsey and the *Enterprise* soon answered Tokyo Rose. They received their orders on 9 January, 1942. *Enterprise* was to join Admiral Fletcher, now embarked on the carrier *Yorktown,* which had recently arrived from the Atlantic, for an offensive strike on Japanese garrisons on the Gilbert and Marshall Islands. Fletcher's forces would hit Jaluit and Mili in the southern Marshalls and Makin in the northern Gilberts; Halsey's planes would strike at Wotje and Maloelap in the northeastern Marshalls as well as at Kwajalein and Roi in the center of this archipelago.

SBD Dauntless squadron approaches the carrier *Enterprise*

The two carriers parted company on 29 January, heading for their respective targets. On board *Enterprise*, Lieutenant Roger W. Mehle, the engineering officer for her fighters, supervised a team of aviation mechanics who were installing armor made of boiler plate behind the seats of all the squadron's Wildcats. At this stage of the war, cockpit armor was not standard in American fighters. *Enterprise*'s fighters were called "Fighting Six" after the number of the carrier.

When the loudspeaker on *Enterprise* blared "Start your engines!" about 4:40 A.M. on 1 February, no one knew quite what the pilots of *Enterprise*'s "main battery" would encounter, but at least they had the assurance of knowing that they would be on the offensive. First Scouting Six and then Bombing Six took off. Their 36 SBDs headed for Roi. Then nine Devastators from Torpedo Six took off for the anchorage at the southern end of the Kwajalein Atoll. The commander of the Kwajalein Attack Group, Commander Howard Young, took off in another SBD, followed by six

STRATEGIC SITUATION IN THE PACIFIC

Allied positions, 1 October 1944
Allied advance to 15 March 1945
Japanese-controlled areas, March 1945

0   200   400   600   800   1000
STATUTE MILES

THE PACIFIC

Wildcats that would fly combat air patrol over the carrier and her escorts. Some time later, six additional fighters took off to hit Maloelap, which was closer than Commander Young's targets.

The pilots' instructions were to hit all targets simultaneously at 6:58 A.M. Although the Japanese had no radar, they were nevertheless ready for the *Enterprise* force when it appeared over Kwajalein. As the SBDs began their glide-bombing runs, they headed right into antiaircraft fire. The Japanese gunners shot down Lieutenant Commander Hallstead Hopping and his tail gunner as they led the attack, but not before they had dropped the first bomb of the war to land on Japanese territory. Despite the loss of their leader, the other pilots of Scouting Six hit Roi heavily, using their 200-pound bombs to blow up buildings, the airfield and an ammunition dump. What the bombs missed, they tried to destroy by strafing from their machine guns.

The attack on the Kwajalein anchorage to the south was just as successful. The big, slow TBD Devastators of Torpedo Six had struck there first, surprising the Japanese and causing considerable damage to the enemy ships anchored behind the atoll's protective coral ring. Then the SBDs arrived. Just as they had practiced, the SBD pilots had climbed for altitude, then pulled up to slow their planes. They split their dive flaps and rolled into a characteristic 70-degree dive. They, too, hit the Japanese hard before retiring. The enemy had less than an hour to recuperate before a third attack of nine Devastators armed with torpedoes arrived over the anchorage. Dodging the Japanese flak, the Devastator pilots went after their targets eagerly. One pilot radioed another, "Get away from that cruiser, Jack! She's mine!" Subsequently, two tankers, a merchantman and the cruiser all took torpedo hits.

Nearby at Maloelap Atoll, Lieutenant Jim Gray led his five fighters in an attack on the airfield, Navy yard and installations there. The attackers caused substantial damage with their 100-pound bombs and machine gun fire, but they ran into trouble with Japanese fighters. Gray at one point was surrounded by a dozen enemy planes, yet he managed to lose them by ducking into a cloud. When he returned to *Enterprise*, the ship's plane handlers were amazed that he had been able to get back. His plane had no rudder control, all of the gasoline in one tank had drained out through a bullet hole, his brakes had been shot away, there was no fuel left in his other tank, and the plane had 30 to 40 bullet holes in it, including one through the propeller. The supply officer on the ship took one look at Gray's plane and remarked that it looked "like the moths had been at it in the attic all summer."

The strikes from *Enterprise* continued for nine hours, with the ship

19

steaming dangerously close to the enemy bases. Thus when one of the dive-bomber pilots was reporting to Admiral Halsey on the bridge, he couldn't help saying, "Admiral, don't you think it's about time we got the hell out of here?"

Halsey, who was well aware of the air and submarine threats that might be nearby, replied, "My boy, I've been thinking the same thing myself." With that, he gave orders to turn eastward and head for Pearl.

When the Japanese finally did try to strike back, the antiaircraft fire of the American ships was very ineffective. In their excitement over firing at live targets, the task force's gunners forgot to lead the enemy planes and instead fired directly at them. Halsey's later evaluation of this effort was characteristically blunt: "Our AA guns might as well have been water pistols." The damage from the bombs the Japanese dropped was minimal—they started a small fire that was quickly extinguished—and they killed one sailor.

The material damage and number of casualties might have been substantial had it not been for the quick thinking and heroics of Aviation

Enterprise launching officer gives the "go" signal

Machinist's Mate Second Class Bruno Peter Gaida. When one Japanese pilot deliberately tried to crash his plane into the ship, Gaida jumped into the rear seat of a Dauntless parked on the flight deck and began firing at the suicide plane. As the Japanese pilot tried to maneuver out of the line of fire of Gaida's twin .30-caliber machine guns, the American's defensive fire continued uninterrupted. Suddenly the attacker's right wing slashed through the tail of Gaida's SBD, nearly hitting him. As the rest of the enemy plane hit the deck, its other wing flew off and crashed into the port catwalk, splashing gasoline over a wide area. What was left of the bomber fell into the sea astern of the ship. Before the day was over, Admiral Halsey acknowledged Gaida's courage with a spot promotion to Aviation Machinist's Mate First Class.

Despite the successes of hit-and-run raids such as the one on the Gilbert and Marshall Islands, the situation in the Pacific was, in the words of President Franklin D. Roosevelt, "very grave." The Japanese had a substantial carrier force consisting of the six Pearl Harbor fleet carriers— *Akagi, Kaga, Soryu, Hiryu, Shokaku* and *Zuikaku*—and four smaller carriers. *Shokaku* and *Zuikaku* were quite new, and at 826 feet in length were powerful warships which carried 72 aircraft and had a maximum speed of 34 knots. The Japanese pilots were experienced and well trained, and in the Zero fighter flew the most maneuverable aircraft in the Pacific in 1942.

The U.S. carrier force was far less powerful. Prior to 1941 the United States had had a modest carrier-building program. Initially, *Enterprise, Lexington, Yorktown* and *Saratoga* were operating in the Pacific. The carriers *Wasp, Hornet* and the small *Ranger* were assigned to the Atlantic Fleet. In April 1942 *Yorktown* was transferred to the Atlantic Fleet with *Hornet* newly arrived in the Pacific. Although the SBD Dauntless was a reliable dive-bomber and the F4F Wildcat an adequate fighter, the TBD Devastator was an old, slow plane which was an easy kill for the Zero. And the Navy's aviators knew it would take time to produce new aircraft that could stay even with or beat the Zero. They also knew pilots, aircrews and carrier crews would have to be trained not only thoroughly but very fast.

Although the U.S. carrier raids on the Gilberts and Marshalls in February 1942 were successful in destroying enemy ships, planes and installations, the United Nations, as the alliance had been named, was suffering serious reverses elsewhere in the Pacific.

Just three days after the war had begun, land-based Japanese G3M Nell bombers had bombed and torpedoed the British battleship *Prince of Wales* and the battle cruiser *Repulse* off the coast of Malaya. These warships had set out to disrupt the Japanese landings prior to an attack on Singapore, but they had done so without any air cover. Their destruction demonstrated convincingly that in the future no capital ship would be safe from a determined aerial attack unless it had an adequate aerial defense and sufficient antiaircraft fire.

More losses followed the sinking of *Prince of Wales* and *Repulse*. After the Japanese had captured Singapore in mid-February, they began a drive to take the oil-rich island of Java. In a last-ditch attempt to reinforce the forces defending Java, USS *Langley*, the U.S. Navy's first aircraft carrier, now converted to a seaplane tender, was dispatched to the island with 32 Army P-40s and their pilots. *Langley* and a freighter that was also carrying aircraft sailed without convoy protection in an attempt to aid the beleaguered American, British, Dutch and Australian forces that were trying to stem the Japanese drive on the island.

Langley never made Java. A Japanese reconnaissance plane spotted the carrier, and in a brief battle with 16 land-based Betty bombers and an equal number of Zeros the *Langley* gamely tried to get through to her destination. But after she had been hit by five bombs and shaken by several near misses, the Americans were forced to abandon the old "Covered Wagon," as she had affectionately been called since her commissioning in 1922.

The Japanese also sank a British carrier, *Hermes*, soon afterward in the Indian Ocean near Ceylon. In this action, Japanese carrier aircraft again demonstrated their effectiveness. Following his return from Pearl Harbor, Admiral Nagumo and four carriers, *Akagi*, *Kaga*, *Shokaku* and *Zuikaku*, had headed south and into the Indian Ocean. In mid-February *Shokaku* and *Zuikaku* had returned to Japan and been replaced by *Soryu* and *Hiryu*. Nagumo's force of four large carriers had raided Port Darwin on the northwest coast of Australia on February 19. Once more Commander Fuchida had led the air attack, which had caused much destruction with small losses.

Following the raid on Port Darwin, Nagumo's force had worked its way westward into the Indian Ocean. Nagumo had then sent *Kaga* home and added *Shokaku* and *Zuikaku*, which had come back from Japan, to his force. Although the British forces in Ceylon and around the Bay of Bengal had put up an aggressive defense, they were no match for the carrier-based attackers. For example, a dive-bomber force of 80 Vals had sunk two British cruisers, *Cornwall* and *Dorsetshire*, in just 19 minutes.

Subsequently Nagumo's patrol planes found the British carrier *Hermes* and destroyer *Vampire*, which had fled Trincomalee, Ceylon, for the greater safety of the open sea. Once more 80 Val dive-bombers attacked two warships. *Hermes* was totally without air cover, because the Japanese had already destroyed her planes while they were parked at the airfields on Ceylon. Fifteen minutes after the attack began, the *Hermes* and her escort had slipped beneath the waves. By then, both had become gutted, flaming wrecks. The Japanese commander of the attack, Lieutenant Commander Takashige Egusa, described the action in two sentences: "It was much simpler than bombing the *Settsu* [the Japanese target battleship used for training naval aviators]. That's all."

With most of the strategic targets in the Indian Ocean destroyed or damaged and the enemy naval forces in the area decimated, Nagumo and his carriers retired northward to Japan. The Japanese land forces were by this time secure in their conquest of Singapore, Java, Borneo, the Netherlands East Indies and the other islands they had attacked in the South Pacific.

While Nagumo and his carriers were operating in the Indian Ocean, U.S. naval forces were conducting limited offensive operations in the South Pacific. Since the earlier raid on the Marshall and Gilbert Islands had been so successful, the basic pattern was repeated against other Japanese-held territories. Thus Vice Admiral Wilson Brown led a task force built around the carrier *Lexington* in a combination air and surface attack on Rabaul, New Britain. When enemy bombers spotted the carrier during her ap-

Captured Japanese Zero with U.S. insignia

USS *Hornet*—a true floating airport

proach, American pilots and antiaircraft fire shot down 16 attackers, five of them being downed by Lieutenant Edward H. ("Butch") O'Hare. Although these losses hurt the Japanese, the failure to achieve surprise blunted Admiral Brown's attack and the task force soon withdrew. Admiral Halsey and *Enterprise* then had their turn as a U.S. Navy task force bombed and shelled the enemy on Wake Island. Eight days later *Enterprise* planes bombed Marcus Island. Total losses for the two operations were two planes.

The fast carrier *Yorktown* joined Admiral Brown and *Lexington* for a raid on the New Guinea ports of Salamaua and Lae in an attempt to slow the Japanese advance toward Australia. This hit-and-run operation caused considerable damage to Japanese warships and transports with only light losses for the American forces. However, it did little to slow the Japanese advance southward.

In contrast to these earlier raids, an exploit in April 1942 achieved almost no significant bomb damage, but it gave a great boost to American morale—and it had some strategic importance. It became famous as the Doolittle Raid. The idea for the raid originated in Washington, when President Roosevelt wondered how the United States could strike back at Japan following Pearl Harbor. Admiral Ernest J. King, Commander in Chief of the U.S. Fleet and Chief of Naval Operations, put his staff to work on the problem. They determined that if long-range Army bombers could be launched from a carrier deck, they could overfly Tokyo from a distance far greater than that of any carrier-based aircraft.

The Japanese high command expected that the Americans might actually try to launch a carrier raid on their homeland. Accordingly, they had stationed a line of small picket boats 500 to 700 miles east of Japan, ranging north and south for 1,000 miles, to give an early warning of approaching attackers. Knowing the range of the U.S. carrier planes, the Japanese leaders reasoned that they could have a defensive force in position to attack the enemy before the American carriers could get close enough to the Home Islands to launch their planes.

What the Japanese hadn't figured into their plans was a man like Lieutenant Colonel James H. Doolittle, who was chosen as commander of the Army Air Corps crews that would make the raid. Doolittle was an exceptional man—aeronautical scientist, holder of several speed records, the first man to fly across the continental United States in 12 hours, the first person to fly the dangerous outside loop, and the first pilot to land a plane blind.

Doolittle and 24 air crews went to Eglin Field, Florida, where they practiced taking off in modified twin-engine B-25 Mitchell bombers from a 500-foot runway that simulated a carrier deck. Of this group, only 16 crews were selected for the mission, and they boarded the fast carrier *Hornet* (commanded by Captain Marc A. Mitscher) in California for the voyage westward. The bombers were loaded onto the same carrier, and she departed for a rendezvous with Admiral Halsey and *Enterprise* north and west of Hawaii. A few minutes before 6:00 A.M. on 12 April, the two fast carriers and their escorts made their rendezvous. The startled sailors on *Enterprise* saw two rows of eight strange planes each on the flight deck of *Hornet*. The planes were parked with their noses angled in toward the center line and their tails and outboard wing tips overhung the sea. The twin rudders and twin engines of the B-25s soon gave the identity of these bombers away.

On this same day Colonel Doolittle told his men, "For the benefit of those who have not already been told or have been guessing, we are going to bomb Japan." Then he outlined the bombing plan. The planes would hit four key Japanese cities—Tokyo, Nagoya, Osaka and Kobe: "The Navy will get us in as close as possible and launch us off the deck." Thirteen planes would each drop four bombs on the Japanese capital. The three remaining planes would individually bomb the other cities. Once their bombs were dropped, the B-25s would continue over Japan to China where they would land behind friendly Chinese lines. When Doolittle asked if anyone wanted to back out, no one stirred.

For the Doolittle plan to work, Halsey would need to get his carriers within 500 miles of Japan. Even after the Army pilots dropped their bombs on Tokyo and the other Japanese cities, they would have to fly another 1,500 miles to the safety of Chinese lines. The plan allowed for a 40-minute reserve of fuel, or enough to fly about 100 miles. Assuming *Hornet* could get close enough to launch the bombers according to the plan, there was also the problem of getting them airborne. A B-25 usually took off at 90 knots on a 3,000-foot runway. The best the pilots could hope for on take-off from the carrier was 60 knots and 800 feet of deck.

Once the two carriers and their escorts had formed up, Halsey sent a terse signal to the other ships which explained everything:

THIS FORCE IS BOUND FOR TOKYO.

While *Hornet* would ferry the bombers westward, planes from *Enterprise* would search ahead of the force—designated Task Force 16—and provide fighter cover overhead. All went well until the early morning hours of 18 April. The radar on *Enterprise* had picked up two surface contacts 10 miles ahead. These were the Japanese picket boats stationed where they could provide an early warning of the enemy's approach. Hoping that his force might not have been spotted in the predawn darkness, Halsey continued to steam westward.

While the American carriers were heading toward Japan, the Army pilots were making their final preparations for their mission. The previous day Captain Mitscher had given Doolittle five Japanese medals that had been awarded to Americans in the past. Two of the recipients had written to the Secretary of the Navy, Frank Knox, and requested that he attach the medals to a bomb "and return [them] to Japan in that manner." Appropri-

Colonel Doolittle and Captain Mitscher on *Hornet*
prior to the mission

ately, Secretary Knox had forwarded the medals to *Hornet*'s skipper. Mitscher and Doolittle then gathered the Army air crews on the flight deck to follow the directions of the medal recipients. They attached the medals to a bomb, which soon bore slogans like "I don't want to set the world on fire, just Tokyo" and "You'll get a BANG out of this!"

With the little ceremony over, the Army crews returned to the details of getting ready for the coming raid. When one of the men asked Colonel Doolittle what they should do if they had to crash-land in Japan, he answered directly. "Each pilot is in command of his own plane when we leave the carrier," he said. "He alone is responsible for the decision he makes for his own plane and crew. Each man must eventually decide for himself what he will do when the chips are down. Personally, I know exactly what I'm going to do."

What was that? Doolittle said, "I don't intend to be taken prisoner. If my plane is crippled beyond any possibility of fighting or escape, I'm going to bail my crew out and then dive it, full throttle, into any target I can find where the crash will do the most damage. I'm 46 years old and have lived a full life. Most of you fellows are in your twenties and if I were you, I'm not sure I would make the same decision. In the final analysis, it's up to each pilot and, in turn, each man to decide what he will do." Soon many of Doolittle's listeners would have to make the very decision that he had already settled for himself.

On the morning following the ceremony with the medals, when an SBD from Bombing Six reported to *Enterprise* that it had been spotted by a Japanese patrol vessel some 50 miles ahead, Admiral Halsey knew he would have to launch the Army bombers far sooner than planned. He couldn't risk the safety of his carriers by steaming to the planned 500-mile launch point. Hence he sent a message to *Hornet* for Doolittle that read:

LAUNCH PLANES X TO COLONEL DOOLITTLE AND HIS GALLANT COM-
MAND GOOD LUCK AND GOD BLESS YOU

HALSEY

The Admiral's decision to launch the B-25s was a wise one. The Japanese fishing boat *Nitto Maru*, stationed 720 miles from Tokyo, had spotted the American warships and reported their presence to the Navy high command. Admiral Yamamoto responded quickly. A look at the charts and a rough calculation showed that the carriers would not be able to get their planes within striking distance of Japan until dawn the next day. The Japanese would have plenty of time to prepare their defenses. Yamamoto ordered a force of battleships, cruisers and destroyers to sea to intercept the enemy. In addition, he sent out 32 medium bombers and a fighter escort of 12 Zeros to locate and destroy the attackers.

Yamamoto's forces never made contact with Task Force 16. The bombers and Zeros flew as far as they could, but there were no American carriers to be found. And the battlewagons never fired a shot at an enemy task force. Instead of reports of an enemy force intercepted and destroyed, Yamamoto received a startling message: "Tokyo bombed!" But where had the bombers come from?

Doolittle had led his planes off *Hornet*'s deck at 8:20 A.M. on 18 April.

28

His plane was the first one off the carrier's deck, 668 miles from Tokyo. The left wing of each bomber hung over the sea as the pilots tried to steer the left wheel down a white line painted on the flight deck. The clearance between the right wing tip and the carrier island was less than 10 feet. Despite gale-force winds and a pitching deck, each pilot managed to get his plane clear of the carrier deck and airborne. The last plane nearly fell into the sea, but somehow the pilot avoided a fatal crash and kept his bomber in the air.

By the time Doolittle reached Tokyo half an hour after noon, the Japanese had just finished a planned air raid drill. No one expected the American bombers yet. There were no fighters in the sky to intercept the Americans and no antiaircraft fire to drive them away. One after another, the Mitchell bombers dropped their explosives on Tokyo. Few residents of the city were even aware that a real air raid was taking place. Except for those in the immediate vicinity of the points where the bombs fell, many of the Japanese who saw the strange planes overhead assumed that they were another part of the air raid drill, something to give it an appearance of realism.

In one of the bombers, Captain Edward York, the pilot, determined that he didn't have enough fuel to get far enough into China to reach the safety of the Chinese lines. Hence he and his crew of five flew northwest to the Soviet city of Vladivostok, where they were interned for the remainder of the war. The other 15 bombers got only as far as Japanese-occupied

B-25 rolls along *Hornet*'s deck

China. Three men died bailing out or crash-landing, and eight were taken prisoner, but the remaining men, including their leader Colonel Doolittle, were alive and heading for Chinese lines.

The Americans that these gallant airmen had left behind got the news that the Doolittle raid was successful indirectly. On *Enterprise* some of the men in radio control were listening to the Tokyo radio station JOAK. In flawless English the announcer was speaking of the joys of living in countries under Japanese domination, when he was interrupted by a torrent of Japanese. Then the station abruptly went off the air. The raid had halted the broadcast for a while. Shortly thereafter, Task Force 16 swung around and headed eastward for the safer waters of Hawaii. For the carriers, this mission was completed.

The handful of bomber pilots that the Japanese captured gave their interrogators a hard time. Their explanation of where they came from varied with each man. Some claimed they had flown from the Aleutians. Others said they had taken off from a special carrier that was unknown to the Japanese. A third explanation involved a mysterious island in the Pacific that was on no map. In contrast to these forced answers, the most famous explanation of where the bombers came from was freely given by a man who had not even gone on the raid, President Roosevelt. He told the press that the bombers had flown from that exotic land of Shangri-La described in James Hilton's novel *Lost Horizon.*

The Japanese eventually got the facts of the raid when they forced the prisoners to reveal the mission of *Hornet* and *Enterprise*. Their determining where the bombers had come from did not, however, alter the fact that Tokyo had been bombed, nor did it dampen the spirits of the Americans who celebrated the Army fliers' method of striking back at a relentless and seemingly invincible foe.

Airborne: B-25 heads for Tokyo

3. Combat—
The Rising Sun

Although the success of the Halsey-Doolittle raid on Tokyo was cause for celebration by Americans, it had hardly been a serious threat to the Japanese capital or a great obstacle to the continuing advance of the Japanese military forces. However, it did cause the Japanese to keep more fighters in the Home Islands for defense against another such raid, which meant that fewer planes could be sent to face the Allies in the South Pacific. Thus it was of some strategic importance. But United States military authorities, particularly Admiral Chester W. Nimitz, the Commander in Chief, Pacific, still had to determine where the Japanese would strike next and what should be done to counter this blow.

Japan had taken Rabaul on New Britain Island in January 1942 and built it into a substantial base from which her pilots could dominate the island chains and open seas to the southeast, south and southwest. Southeast of Rabaul lay the Australian base of Tulagi in the Solomons archipelago. Due south was the Coral Sea, the direct ocean pathway to northern Australia. Port Moresby, the Australian base in Papua, which is part of the island of New Guinea, was situated to the southwest of Rabaul. Nimitz knew that this was the general direction in which the Japanese would move, but he needed more specific information in order for the U.S. Navy to be in the right place at the right time to intercept.

Fortunately, Magic, the American intelligence operation that was reading the Japanese diplomatic and naval codes, had revealed the broad outlines of the Japanese plan. By mid-April 1942 Admiral Nimitz was able to direct a two-carrier task force commanded by Rear Admiral Frank Jack Fletcher to the Coral Sea to stop the Japanese.

The Japanese plan for an advance on Australia was complicated. They would send three separate forces into the area. One force would take Tulagi, establish a seaplane base there, and then begin attacks on the American base at Nouméa farther to the south on New Caledonia. A second force would capture the Allied base at Port Moresby, the logical jumping-off point for a future invasion of Australia. This force would consist of a substantial army carried on 14 transports and protected by light cruisers and the light carrier *Shoho*. The third force was composed of two fast carriers, *Shokaku* and *Zuikaku*, and their escorts. Vice Admiral Takeo Takagi commanded this carrier force, and his orders from the senior commander in the area, Vice Admiral Shigeyoshi Inouye, Commander in Chief Fourth Fleet, were straightforward: destroy any forces that the United States and her allies might use to interfere with these Japanese operations in the Coral Sea. Operation Mo, as the Japanese labeled their plan, was the key to a successful invasion of New Caledonia and Fiji in July, which would then be followed by carrier strikes and an invasion of Australia in August.

Admiral Fletcher's carrier task force was outgunned and outmanned relative to the Japanese, but it did have knowledge of the enemy's general intentions and it had the desire to strike back in a decisive fleet action. As task force commander, Fletcher, an old battleship sailor, was embarked on the carrier *Yorktown*. An experienced aviator, Rear Admiral Aubrey W. Fitch, who was in the other carrier, *Lexington*, commanded the carrier division. Rear Admiral Thomas C. Kinkaid was in charge of the cruisers and destroyers that screened the carriers against air, surface and submarine attack. An additional Allied naval force that had been supporting General MacArthur was also under Fletcher's command. This force, consisting of two Australian and one U.S. cruiser and a few destroyers, was commanded by Rear Admiral J. G. Crace, RN.

The battle opened with the Japanese occupying Tulagi with no opposition on 3 May. The next day planes from *Yorktown* carried out an air strike on that newly taken Japanese base, but they caused only slight damage. Although the Americans had given the Japanese notice that they were in the Coral Sea with this attack on Tulagi, the Japanese carriers were not yet able to strike back because they were too far away. For the next two days,

Admiral Nimitz

Fletcher and Takagi warily searched for each other with land-based and carrier air patrols. At one point the two carrier task forces were as close as 70 miles, but this was at night when air patrols were not flown, even under possible battle conditions. Elsewhere in the Pacific on 6 May 1942, conditions were not so peaceful; the Japanese had just accepted General Jonathan M. Wainwright's surrender of Corregidor in the Philippines.

The pace of battle picked up on 7 May, when search planes from the Japanese carriers *Shokaku* and *Zuikaku* spotted Fletcher's oiler *Neosho* and her escort, the single-stack destroyer *Sims*, which were withdrawing from the potential battle area. The Japanese search planes erroneously reported that they had found a carrier and a cruiser. Eager to attack an enemy carrier, Rear Admiral Chuichi Hara, who was Takagi's carrier division commander, ordered a full-scale bombing attack on *Neosho* and *Sims*.

When the oiler and her escort realized shortly after 9:00 that morning that they were in for an attack in force, the oiler's skipper, Captain John S. Phillips, cranked his ship up to flank speed of 18 knots and began evasive

33

maneuvering in an attempt to throw off the aim of the Japanese pilots. At the same time, *Sims* kept pace with her charge's erratic course.

To counter these efforts, the Japanese bombers split into two groups in preparation for horizontal bombing runs. As the bombers approached, the antiaircraft guns on the two American ships began to fire, but Captain Phillips calmly waited to see where the bombs were headed. Once the Japanese had let go their deadly missiles, he abruptly changed course again. The bombs all missed. *Sims,* too, had escaped for the moment with only minor injuries to the shoulder of one sailor.

At that point the situation began to deteriorate. First, Captain Phillips ordered his communications officer to radio Admiral Fletcher that they were under attack from Japanese carrier planes. Somehow the message never got through to the task force commander; thus he continued searching for the Japanese, unaware that their two fast carriers were steaming to the north of him.

Thwarted by the American defensive efforts in this initial attack, the Japanese broke off the engagement to regroup and rearm. They returned about noon, intent upon destroying the enemy "carrier." They attacked in three waves. Violent maneuvering by *Sims* and *Neosho* as well as furious antiaircraft fire was no longer enough. *Sims* took at least three direct hits from 500-pound bombs and was soon sinking. As the ship began to break in two, the surviving members of the *Sims* crew hastily abandoned ship in whatever boats and rafts they could get afloat.

Neosho was not much better off. She took seven direct bomb hits, but the "Fat Lady," as the sailors jokingly referred to her, stayed afloat owing to the buoyancy provided by her undamaged fuel tanks. *Neosho* soon lost all power and began to drift with the sea. With no place else to go, the survivors from *Sims* quickly made for the battered oiler. Without power and low on food, water and medical supplies for her injured men, the derelict *Neosho* floated for four days as sea water slowly began to fill her interior. Fortunately, the destroyer *Henley,* which was part of a sea-air search team, found the oiler on 11 May and rescued 109 survivors of *Neosho* and 14 men from *Sims. Henley* then tried to sink the Fat Lady with torpedoes, but these weapons were so defective that the destroyer finally had to fire 146 rounds of 5-inch ammunition into the oiler before she would go down.

While the Japanese were expending substantial time and effort to sink *Sims* and *Neosho,* the American carrier planes were also being misled. A *Yorktown* search plane had reported sighting "two carriers and four heavy cruisers" some 175 miles northwest of Task Force 17 on the morning of 7 May. Admiral Fletcher interpreted this report to be a sighting of the Japanese carrier force he was after. He ordered a full strike into the air to attack. Only after the American planes were on their way toward the enemy did Fletcher get a corrected report indicating "two heavy cruisers and two destroyers." (Actually the contact was two old light cruisers, three converted gunboats and a seaplane tender.) By coincidence, however, the American planes found bigger game—the Japanese light carrier *Shoho*—only 35 miles away.

Lexington's group consisted of 10 fighters, 28 dive-bombers and 12 torpedo bombers. The *Yorktown* planes, which arrived over *Shoho* somewhat later than those of "Lady Lex," included 8 fighters, 7 dive-bombers, 17 SBDs and 10 torpedo planes. *Shoho's* mission in Operation Mo was to provide air cover for the 14 Japanese transports in the invasion force. Thus most of her fighters were off flying patrols for the invasion force when the Americans arrived overhead.

F4F is moved into position on a carrier flight deck

Lieutenant Commander John ("Jimmy") Thach,
inventor of the "Thach weave" maneuver

Although Captain Ishonosuke Izawa, commander of *Shoho*, launched what fighters he could and began violently zigzagging his ship to throw off the Americans' aim, these efforts were not enough to protect the carrier against more than 90 U.S. aircraft. Attacking from several directions, the Americans pounded *Shoho*. Two bombs hit the rear elevator on the flight deck, several torpedoes smashed into the vessel's stern on the starboard side, and then more bombs and torpedoes found their mark. Soon the carrier had lost all power and steering. Fires fed by the gasoline and weapons stored inside the ship raged through the vessel's internal compartments. Without power, without steerageway, and dead in the water, the Japanese defenders continued to fire as best they could at the American planes. In Stanley Johnston's *Queen of the Flat-Tops*, Lieutenant Commander Jim Flatley, skipper of *Yorktown*'s fighters, described what the action was like:

> I was sitting upstairs at 5,000 feet watching them come down. The heavy bombs began exploding at three and four second intervals. Fire, flames, and

sea water were being thrown hundreds of feet high, from each explosion. The 1,000-pound bombs seemed to be pattering down like rain and those big babies do four times as much damage as the 500 pounders.

The sight of those heavy bombs smashing that carrier was so awful it gave me a sick feeling. Every second bomb was landing and exploding aboard the ship. Those powerful blasts were literally tearing the big ship apart. She burst into flames from bow to stern. I don't see how anybody aboard that ship could have survived.

According to knowledgeable Japanese officers who were participants in the battle, *Shoho* capsized within five minutes of taking her first bomb hit. That bomb may have been dropped by Lieutenant Commander Weldon Hamilton of *Lexington*. He led that carrier's dive-bombers in the attack. After the attack, Hamilton reported that his 1,000-pound bomb was the first to hit *Shoho,* and he said that it "struck in the middle of the flight deck's width, just abaft of amidships. As I looked back, the entire after portion of the flight deck was ablaze and pouring forth heavy black smoke." Whether Hamilton was the first pilot to hit *Shoho* is less important than the fact that the carrier staggered from 13 bomb and seven torpedo hits in the brief battle. For those carrier men awaiting news of the outcome of the attack, *Lexington*'s Lieutenant Commander Robert E. Dixon summed up the victory very concisely when he radioed: "Dixon to carrier. Scratch one flattop!"

The loss of *Shoho* put Admirals Takagi and Hara in a bind. They could not let her go unavenged, yet the day was growing late, with rain squalls and low visibility complicating the problem of finding the enemy carriers. At 4:30 P.M. Lieutenant Commander Kakuichi Tukahashi got his orders to find the Americans and attack at twilight. Tukahashi was a veteran of Pearl Harbor and he had led the attack on *Neosho* and *Sims* earlier in the day. This time he took off with only 12 dive-bombers and 15 torpedo bombers, all of which were piloted by his most experienced airmen.

The heavy rain squalls, blanketing clouds and growing twilight hid the enemy carriers from Tukahashi and his fellow pilots, and he finally ordered his men to jettison their bombs and torpedoes to make the flight home easier. While searching for their own carriers, the Japanese pilots blindly came within range of *Lexington*'s radar. Her air control officer vectored the local fighter patrol in the direction of the Japanese Vals and Kates. In the ensuing melee, the American pilots in their Grumman Wildcats shot down eight torpedo bombers and one dive-bomber.

Shortly thereafter one Japanese pilot, who was probably approaching exhaustion, mistook *Yorktown* for *Zuikaku*. Switching on his lights in preparation for landing, the pilot and each of the eight other bombers with him began their descent to land. When the Japanese pilot realized he was headed for the wrong flight deck, he took off in a hurry. The surprised Americans fired back, but without success.

The second time the Japanese pilots mistook an American carrier for one of their own that night, the outcome was different. The Americans did manage to shoot down one enemy plane. When the remaining Japanese planes finally found their carriers, more planes were lost in the night recovery operations. Only six planes returned safely. Although Commander Tukahashi had lost most of his force in the abortive twilight attack, he did accomplish one part of his mission—he had located *Yorktown* and *Lexington* with certainty. Hence all four admirals—Fletcher and Fitch, Takagi and Hara—knew that 8 May would bring the battle that both sides had been looking for.

Both carrier forces flew reconnaissance planes off their decks early the next morning. Flight Warrant Officer Kenzo Kanno found and shadowed the American task force, reporting its position, composition and movements by radio to *Shokaku*. Similarly, an American scout found the Japanese carriers. Once more Tukahashi led the Japanese attack, which consisted of 18 fighters, 33 dive-bombers and 18 torpedo bombers. The Americans launched their counterattack with 39 planes from *Yorktown* under Lieutenant Commander Joe Taylor of Torpedo Squadron 5. *Lexington*'s 46 planes followed some time later.

The two carrier forces were evenly matched. Each had two fast carriers. The Japanese, with 122 planes available, had only one more than the Americans. Where *Yorktown* and *Lexington* were stronger in bombers, the Japanese had more fighter and torpedo planes. The Japanese pilots had more combat experience and more reliable torpedoes, but the Americans had radar. One other difference, an important one, existed that day. The American ships were steaming in bright tropical sunlight, but the Japanese carriers, 235 miles away, were in an area of rain squalls and clouds which hampered visibility greatly.

Lieutenant Commander Dixon had provided sufficient reconnaissance information that the first *Yorktown* planes found the Japanese without trouble. While *Zuikaku* headed for cover under a rain squall, *Shokaku* began to launch more fighters for protective cover. Joe Taylor and his torpedo squadron planned to hit the Japanese from on high—17,000 feet— with dive-bombers and low with torpedo bombers. *Shokaku* began evasive maneuvers when confronted by the American attack, but this was not enough. The *Yorktown* pilots got two bomb hits (though they claimed six bomb and three torpedo hits). The American torpedoes were launched too far away; consequently they either missed or failed to explode upon impact.

But one bomb caused considerable damage. It hit the Japanese carrier well forward on the starboard bow and ignited gasoline in the area and damaged the flight deck. The other bomb hit well aft on the vessel. Despite these casualties, the *Shokaku* could still recover aircraft even though she could no longer launch them.

Excited by the success of the attack, Commander Taylor announced—as reported by Edwin P. Hoyt—the extent of the damage to the enemy carrier quite graphically:

> "The area on the port side from the bow aft for about 50 to 100 feet was one mass of flames from the waterline to the flight deck. The flame was exceptionally intense. It looked like that from an acetylene torch, and appeared to be coming from inside the ship. Another small fire was burning at the starboard quarter. When the carrier was last seen . . . the fires were burning fiercely. It is believed probable that this carrier was so badly damaged that it finally sank."

Gratifying as this scene must have been to Commander Taylor and his fellow pilots, it was inaccurate, at least in its conclusion. Even though the late-arriving *Lexington* group added another bomb hit to the two from *Yorktown*, *Shokaku* was not sunk at the Coral Sea. She lost 108 men killed and 40 wounded, but the fires were quickly brought under control, none of the torpedoes had damaged the carrier below the waterline, and many of the planes were able to transfer to *Zuikaku*, which had survived the American attack with only minor damage. Although damaged and unable to launch planes, *Shokaku* was still afloat. Admiral Takagi released her with orders to return to Japan for repairs.

With their strike completed, the Americans, especially the late arrivals from *Lexington*, still had to fly back home. At least 20 Zeros were there to make the long flight back very difficult. One by one, the American planes fought off attacks from the faster and more maneuverable Zeros. Some were shot down. Others, like Commander William B. Ault, who led *Lexington*'s dive-bomber squadron, avoided the Zeros but ran out of gas on the way home.

At one point, Ault radioed *Lexington:* "Can you hear me and do you have me on the [radar] screen? I have gas left for about 20 minutes."

The reply was brief. "I can hear you. You are not on screen."

Ault tried once more: "Shall I circle? Do you want me to gain or lose altitude? I have gas left for about 20 minutes."

The reply: "You are not on the screen. Try to make the nearest land."

Ault's answer was realistic: "Nearest land is over 200 miles away. We would never make it."

The carrier responded, "You are on your own. Good luck."

Ault then radioed in that he believed he had made a 1,000-pound-

Thach (foreground) and Lieutenant E. H.
("Butch") O'Hare starred in early air battles

bomb hit on a Japanese carrier and that he was heading north. The carrier's last transmission to him was another wish for his good luck. Bill Ault was never heard from again.

Between the time that *Yorktown*'s planes made their attack on *Shokaku* and the arrival of the group from *Lexington* over the Japanese carrier, the Japanese attack group of 90 planes had found *Lexington* and *Yorktown*. Approaching from the northeastward, which was down wind and down sun, the enemy planes were eager to attack. One reason they found the American carriers without difficulty was the work of Flight Warrant Officer Kenzo Kanno. He not only shadowed the carriers, radioing back their position and movements, but he also deliberately led the attackers to the carriers, even though that meant he would lack sufficient fuel to return to his own ship.

The Japanese planes went for *Yorktown* first. They had little air opposition en route to the carriers because the Americans' combat air patrol was inadequate in numbers and it met the Japanese too close to the carriers. All the carriers and their escorts could do was depend on their own antiaircraft fire to protect themselves.

Kanno and then Tukahashi dived on *Yorktown*. Both were shot down within seconds, but other pilots got through. The sky was filled with diving, dodging aircraft and hundreds of black puffs caused by exploding antiaircraft shells. The sea below boiled with the angry wakes of ships at flank speed trying to avoid bombs, torpedoes or enemy planes. Exploding bombs and shrapnel added to the turmoil on the surface.

The leader of *Zuikaku*'s air group, Lieutenant Commander Shigekazu Shimazaki, later explained to Masatake Okumiya and Jino Harikoshi what he felt during the battle:

> "Never in all my years in combat had I ever imagined a battle like this! Our fighters and American Wildcats dived and climbed in the middle of formations.
>
> Burning and shattered planes of both sides plunged from the skies. Amidst this fantastic rainfall of antiaircraft shells and spinning planes, I dived almost to the water's surface and sent my torpedo into *Lexington*.
>
> I had to fly just above the waves to escape the enemy shells. I was flying below the level of the flight deck and I almost struck the bow of the ship. I could see American sailors staring at my plane as it rushed by."

Although *Yorktown* was attacked from the stern by torpedo bombers and then by dive-bombers, she took only a single bomb hit. This 800-pound bomb, however, caused plenty of damage. It hit the carrier's flight deck some 15 feet inboard of the island and penetrated to the fourth deck below the flight deck. There, in the bowels of the ship, it started fires and killed or injured 66 men, mostly from burns.

Lexington was not so fortunate. The Japanese torpedo bombers came

Japanese torpedo bomber—the Nakajima
B5N2, code-named Kate

at her on both sides of her bow. Thus there was no direction in which Captain Frederick C. ("Ted") Sherman could turn to escape undamaged. Sherman's problems were compounded by the ponderous maneuverability of Lady Lex. She could not avoid the torpedoes the way the smaller *Yorktown* had.

The first torpedo hit *Lexington* on the port side forward. A second struck her on the starboard side near the bridge. This damage was compounded by bomb hits in a 5-inch ready-ammunition locker forward and in the smokestack structure. Several near misses jarred the big ship, rupturing plates in the vessel's hull and throwing up mountains of water.

On *Lexington*, Yeoman Third Class Charles Dorton saw the attack in vivid terms:

> The pilots of the Japanese torpedo planes seemed nervous. You could see them plainly as they swept in towards the ship through our machine-gun fire.

> Things began to happen fast. Antiaircraft racket was awful. The sky was filled with shrapnel. One Japanese torpedo plane was hit by our machine-gun fire when it was 200 yards away. And only sixty feet above the water. The Japanese didn't have a chance to launch his "fish" but turned and kept coming right at us. He crashed into the ship near the port forward gun battery. Our boys quickly shoved the wreck off into the water before it could catch fire and explode the torpedo.

Smoke gives *Lexington*'s deck a foggy appearance

Only about 20 minutes had elapsed between the first attack and the end of the battle. Yet plenty of damage had been done. Tukahashi's second in command subsequently reported to his superiors that "at least nine torpedoes and more than ten 550-pound bombs struck the [Lexington], while [the Yorktown] was hit with three torpedoes and eight to ten 550-pound bombs. We damaged two other vessels." In reality, the score was somewhat less. Two torpedoes and two bombs hit Lexington, while one bomb hit Yorktown. Both ships received several near misses.

Admiral Takagi received the pilots' reports of one large and one medium American carrier sunk and one battleship or cruiser left burning as sufficient evidence of victory. Yet his forces had not come away without their own losses. Post-battle analysis established that the Japanese lost a total of 43 aircraft from all causes, while Task Force 17 lost 33 planes. Additionally, Zuikaku had only 24 fighters, 9 dive-bombers and 6 torpedo bombers operational at the end of the day. The Japanese also had to consider their losses of experienced pilots. Men like Kanno and Tukahashi would not be easily replaced.

On the basis of battle reports he had received, the Japanese naval commander, Admiral Inouye, ordered Admiral Takagi to retire with his carrier forces to Truk. Inouye also decided to postpone the Port Moresby invasion until July because he was afraid to risk his transports against the planes of the Army Air Forces without the air cover supplied by Shoho. Thus Task Force 17 had effectively stalled the Japanese advance into the Coral Sea and the invasion of Port Moresby.

Although these movements of the Japanese forces were predicated upon the sinking of Lexington and Yorktown, the action in the Coral Sea did not end with the departure of the Japanese planes around noon on 8 May. Lexington was damaged seriously by both bombs and torpedoes, but she managed to recover her aircraft following the attack. Lieutenant Noel Gayler, for example, landed to report that he had downed two more Japanese planes to raise his total number of kills to eight.

Initially the reports to Captain Sherman on the damage below decks were encouraging. The damage control parties were working hard to isolate the flooded compartments, shore up weakened bulkheads and put out fires. Shortly after noon Admiral Fitch, who was embarked on Lexington, radioed Admiral Fletcher that Lexington's maximum speed was 24 knots despite the damage below decks. Lieutenant Commander H. R. Healy, the carrier's damage control officer, reported to Captain Sherman the satisfactory state of repairs: "We've got the torpedo damage temporarily shored up, the fires out and soon will have the ship back on an even keel. But I

43

would suggest, sir, that if you have to take any more torpedoes, you take 'em on the starboard side."

Although Healy may have been speaking somewhat facetiously, all seemed to be going well on *Lexington* until 12:47 P.M., when a huge internal explosion rocked the ship. At first, the bridge watch thought that a 1,000-pound bomb that had failed to explode on impact had suddenly blown up. In fact, that was not the cause. Someone had left a motor generator running following the attack, and it had ignited gasoline vapors released by one of the torpedo hits.

Fires and smoke quickly filled many of the ship's spaces. More explosions followed. Debris flew in all directions. The blasts tore steel doors off their hinges as though they were matchbook covers. The first blast had killed Commander Healy in the damage control central station and killed or injured scores of others. When the day was finally over for *Lexington*, more of her men had died from these explosions than had been killed in the Japanese attack.

Despite the new damage, the ship still looked as if she would survive. The last *Lexington* plane touched down at 2:14 P.M. with the ship making 25 knots. But about half an hour later, a second major internal explosion wrecked the ventilation system in the ship's fire and engine rooms, disrupted communications and knocked out key fire mains throughout the ship. Fighting the fires now became exceedingly difficult. At 2:56 Captain Sherman ordered a signal raised on the carrier's flag hoist which would alert the task force to his problems. That signal simply stated, "This ship needs help." The task force opened up its formation to give *Lexington* plenty of room. By that time, the carrier's bridge watch had lost all steering control and emergency steering had passed to men operating the hand wheels aft in the bowels of the ship near the huge rudders. When all means of communication from bridge to after steering subsequently failed, Captain Sherman had to rely upon a human chain to pass the helm orders aft and down 400 feet to the steersmen in the after engineering spaces who would physically move the ship's rudders.

Even with the destroyer *Morris* alongside to provide fire-fighting pumps and assistance, the situation continued to deteriorate. Temperatures in the ship's engineering spaces had reached 160 degrees, hot enough to blister the paint on the bulkheads. Sherman received reports that warheads stored on the hangar decks had reached 140 degrees and were in danger of blowing up. Accordingly, he ordered the engineers, the "black gang," to secure the engineering plant and to get up on deck. With the rush of escaping steam from the safety valves, the ship lost all power and went dead in the water about 4:30 P.M. Shortly after 5:00, Admiral Fitch called down

Lexington is mortally wounded

to Captain Sherman and said, "Well, Ted, let's get the men off." With that, all hands prepared to abandon ship. Rafts were cast loose, boats from the escorts standing by picked up men who climbed down to the water on knotted lines, and searches were made to be sure that all the wounded and other personnel below decks had gotten the word to leave.

Captain Sherman later described the situation in this way:

It was heartbreaking, but it seemed to be the only thing left to do. Reluctantly I gave the order to abandon ship. It was the hardest thing I have ever done. Nevertheless, if we could not prevent the loss of the *Lexington*, saving the lives of the crew was of utmost importance.

The officers and men were as reluctant to leave as I was. We had to order them to go. Most of the wounded were lowered to a destroyer alongside . . . Some of the crew, while waiting to disembark . . . [got some ice cream and] stood around the flight deck eating it. . . . Some of them lined up their shoes in orderly fashion on the deck before they left, as if they expected to return. There was not the slightest panic or disorder. I was proud of them.

Finally, when all the men had left, the captain made one final tour of topside spaces to make sure all the wounded had been transferred. Then he followed his executive officer down a line to the water, where they were dragged aboard a waiting whaleboat. As they left the ship, more explosions followed, hurling debris in all directions.

By 6:00 P.M. *Lexington* was listing about 30 degrees to port. Smoke continued to pour out of the ship. Admiral Fletcher then gave the order to torpedo Lady Lex. She had now become a burden by lighting up the sky for any enemy planes or submarines to see the task force. Just short of 8:00 P.M., the destroyer *Phelps* delivered the final blow which sent the great carrier to the bottom. As she went down, *Lexington* was once more rent by great explosions and detonations.

Jack Smith, a *Lexington* sailor, was there when she went down: "I couldn't watch her go, and men who had been with her since she was commissioned in '27 stood with tears streaming." With her sinking, *Lexington* carried down the bodies of 216 men and the remains of 36 planes, but 19 planes had earlier been transferred to *Yorktown* and 2,735 men were picked up by the screening ships in Task Force 17.

With the sinking of *Lexington*, Admiral Fletcher and his task force departed from the Coral Sea. *Yorktown* returned to Hawaii to be repaired. The other ships and men of the task force went on to new missions and jobs. The Japanese had won a tactical victory in the Coral Sea since they had lost only *Shoho* as against the American losses of *Sims*, *Neosho* and *Lexington*, but Fletcher's forces had also achieved valuable goals. They had turned back the Japanese invasion of the Coral Sea and Port Moresby. They had damaged *Shokaku* and *Zuikaku* sufficiently to make them unavailable for any future combat for one to two months. Although no one could yet know it, that meant that both would miss the coming Battle of Midway.

And *Lexington* and her crew had convincingly demonstrated that the carrier was not the vulnerable warship its critics had claimed. Instead *Lexington* had proved that when properly fought and operated, a carrier could absorb great damage from either bombs or torpedoes. That kind of toughness was exactly the quality the American naval forces would need at Midway.

Admiral Nagumo's flagship, the
carrier *Akagi*

4. Combat-
Give and Take

The day, 27 May, was special in Japan—Navy Day, the anniversary of Admiral Togo's magnificent victory over the Russian fleet in the Battle of Tsushima during the Russo-Japanese War. On Navy Day in 1942 another Japanese fleet, the First Carrier Striking Force, commanded by Vice Admiral Chuichi Nagumo, got under way from the fleet anchorage at Hashirajima in the Inland Sea of Japan for what many Japanese leaders expected would be another great victory: the invasion of Midway Island and the destruction of the United States fleet.

At 8:00 A.M. a single signal flag on the flagship of the Nagumo Force, as it was called, ordered the fleet into action: "Sortie as scheduled." Aboard Nagumo's flagship, the fast carrier *Akagi*, Captain Mitsuo Fuchida experienced the exhilaration of the moment:

"As we steamed out of the anchorage the ships of the other forces, which would sortie two days later, gave us a roaring send-off. The crews lined the rails and cheered and waved their caps as we passed. They seemed to envy our good fortune in being the first to leave. We waved back a farewell, and a gen-

eral gaiety prevailed. Every man was convinced that he was about to partici-
pate in yet another brilliant victory."

The "other forces" that Captain Fuchida saw were equally as formidable and impressive as Nagumo's four fast carriers—*Akagi, Soryu, Kaga* and
Hiryu—and their escorts of battleships, cruisers and destroyers. One of the
other forces at Hashirajima was the Japanese battleship fleet composed of
seven dreadnoughts under the overall command of Admiral Isoroku Yamamoto, the Commander in Chief of the Japanese Combined Fleet. Yamamoto's flagship was the battleship *Yamato*, the biggest battleship then
afloat at 68,000 tons and armed with 18.1-inch guns. Also at Hashirajima
was a force commanded by Vice Admiral Nobutake Kondo with two battleships, four heavy cruisers, one light cruiser, the light carrier *Zuiho* and
eight destroyers.

Collectively, this gray armada shared one objective, the capture of
Midway and the destruction of the enemy fleet, but it had several individual missions. Kondo's force, for example, was part of a fleet that would pro-
tect the landings on Midway once all enemy air and surface opposition had
been neutralized. Nagumo's carriers were to fly air strikes against the
Americans at Midway and any enemy fleet that might appear to oppose the
Japanese advance. The battleship force, or Main Force, was also there to
take on enemy surface forces and to ensure that the impending assault on
Midway was successful. The only Japanese forces that did not sortie from
Hashirajima in late May 1942 were a fleet of 26 ships, including the light
carrier *Ryujo* and carrier *Junyo*, assigned to attack American bases in the
Aleutian Island chain off the Alaskan mainland and the nearly 50-ship force
that would actually land troops on Midway. These transports and their escorts would sortie from Saipan and Guam and steam independently to
Midway.

The Japanese plan was extraordinarily complex. The Aleutians attack
was designed as a feint which would divert American attention away from
Midway and the Central Pacific. Thus Rear Admiral Kakuji Kakuta's Second Carrier Striking Force (a part of the Japanese Northern Force) would
carry out air strikes to neutralize Dutch Harbor, the major American base
in the Aleutians, on 4 June and follow this up with landings at Adak and
Kiska Islands two days later.

In the meantime, the other Japanese forces would concentrate on
Midway, with the main landings scheduled for 7 June. A preinvasion air
strike from Nagumo's First Carrier Striking Force would knock out U.S. air
and sea forces in the Midway area. Following the landings on 7 June,
Yamamoto's battleship force (the Main Body), the Nagumo Force and

Obsolescent Brewster Buffalos like this one defended Midway

Patrol plane crew that spotted the Japanese approaching Midway

other Japanese forces would position themselves to repel the expected American counterattack. *Yamato* and the other battleships were supposed to deliver a crushing blow to the U.S. naval forces that undoubtedly would be rushing westward from Hawaii to try to regain Midway.

Why was Midway—this small coral atoll less than six miles in diameter, made up of two tiny islets surrounding a clear, blue lagoon—the center of so much interest? The Japanese decided to attack Midway in part because it lay only 1,136 miles west of Hawaii. Although the Americans used it only as a base from which they flew air patrols, Admiral Chester W. Nimitz and the U.S. Navy could not afford to have Japanese forces permanently stationed so close to Hawaii. Yet the Japanese reasoning behind their plan involved more than the proximity of Midway to Pearl Harbor. Despite the strategic loss they suffered in the Battle of the Coral Sea, the Japanese naval leadership considered that to have been a minor setback when weighed against the string of victories elsewhere in the South Pacific and Indian Oceans. Commander Minoru Genda, an experienced aviator who was then the operations officer on Nagumo's staff, summed up the prevailing attitude in Tokyo when he commented on the Midway plan that Yamamoto and his staff "still think that the initiative is entirely in our hands."

In addition to believing that they still held the initiative in the war, the Japanese naval leadership, particularly Admiral Yamamoto, also chose to attack Midway and the Aleutians because of the Halsey-Doolittle raid on Tokyo in April 1942. Even though Naval General Staff dismissed the attack as a "do-nothing" raid, it had shown that all of Yamamoto's precautions against an attack on the Japanese homeland had been inadequate. The raid had hurt Yamamoto's pride as well. Therefore he would destroy the carriers that had launched the attack and push the Japanese defensive perimeter eastward to a north-south line from the Aleutians to Midway. Here, then, was one of the key strategic effects of the Doolittle raid.

Strategically, a Japanese attack on Midway actually had more justification that halting hit-and-run raids on Tokyo. Genda and others had argued convincingly that the next objective for the Japanese Navy had to be the destruction of the enemy carriers that they had missed at Pearl Harbor. An attack on Midway would be such a direct threat to the security of Hawaii that Nimitz would have to commit his carriers in defense. Once the U.S. fleet was drawn into battle, the Japanese planners were confident their forces would be the victors.

Some senior officers argued that a better way to achieve this goal would be to cut the lines of supply and communication between Hawaii and Australia. Yamamoto opposed this method of dealing with the American fleet. He is reported by Captain Fuchida to have expressed his opinion unequivocally in favor of an attack on Midway, saying,

> "We believe that by launching the proposed operations against Midway, we can succeed in drawing out the enemy's carrier strength and destroying it in decisive battle. If, on the other hand, the enemy should avoid our challenge, we shall still realize an important gain by advancing our defensive perimeter to Midway and the western Aleutians without obstruction."

There were certain problems with the Midway plan that were pointed out prior to the sortie from Hashirajima. One was the sheer number of ships and men involved—more than 150 warships and their crews, as well as the 5,000 soldiers on the transports in the Invasion Force. Added to this was the coordination of operations involving the Northern Force's attack on the Aleutians, Nagumo's carrier strikes, the protection of the transport force and the destruction of the enemy fleet by Yamamoto's Main Force.

The Japanese believed these problems could be overcome through planning and luck. But another danger, one that could be identified only in retrospect, was also present in the plan. According to Captain Fuchida and Commander Masatohe Okumiya, Yamamoto and his staff planners "completely failed to provide for the contingency that the enemy might somehow learn of our intentions in advance and thus be able to deploy his forces for an ambush attack." Fuchida and Okumiya ascribe this oversight to the "arrogant overconfidence" engendered by Japan's early victories in the war. Although their point may hold considerable truth about why the battle ultimately turned out as it did, it alone does not entirely account for some of the tactical decisions made by Nagumo during the heat of the battle. Perhaps an even more serious flaw than the plan's failure to provide for an unexpected attack by enemy carrier forces was the wording of the sailing orders given to Nagumo. The Commander of the First Carrier Striking Force had, say Fuchida and Okumiya, "been assigned two tactical missions which were essentially incompatible. The assignment to attack Midway on 5 June in preparation for the landing operation put his force under rigid limitations of movement. The other mission—to contact and destroy enemy naval forces—required that Nagumo be entirely free to move as the situation required, and it also made it absolutely essential to keep our whereabouts secret while searching for the enemy." Yet Yamamoto and his staff never indicated which of these two missions should have precedence over the other. This flaw in the Japanese plan, more than any other, would contribute directly to the loss of four of Japan's fast carriers at Midway.

While the Japanese were planning their attack on Midway, Admiral Nimitz and his staff at Pearl Harbor were making their own plans to counter the expected enemy offensive. Because the Magic intelligence operation permitted American cryptographers to read the Japanese code, Nimitz and other high officials in Washington knew that the Japanese were planning a major attack. What they weren't sure of was the target of the attack, because the Japanese always referred to the target as AF. Some people thought AF was Alaska, or Hawaii, or the West Coast, but Nimitz figured it was Midway.

To pin the identity of AF down, Nimitz had the base commander at Midway issue a fake uncoded radio message stating that Midway's freshwater machinery had broken down. Shortly thereafter the cryptographers at Pearl Harbor intercepted a Japanese message reporting that AF was low on fresh water. So by mid-May, Nimitz was sure where the Japanese were going to attack. By 25 May his combat intelligence unit had even pieced together which Japanese ships and units would be participating in the operation, what courses they would take to Midway, and the approximate date of attack, 3–5 June.

While the cryptographers were reading the Japanese code, Nimitz had moved to reinforce Midway and to assemble a carrier task force to oppose the attack. By 4 June the two tiny islets at Midway bulged with 120 aircraft belonging to the Marines, Navy and Army (B-17s and B-26s), 11 PT boats, 5 tanks, 8 mortars, 14 shore-defense guns, 32 antiaircraft guns and 3,632 defenders from the three services. The crush of men and material on the island caused one marine to joke that Midway looked "like an asparagus patch."

The fleet that Nimitz assembled was hardly as big or as impressive as the one Yamamoto had ordered to sea on 27 May. In mid-May Rear Admiral Frank Jack Fletcher in *Yorktown* with Task Force 17 was at Tongatabu, in the Tonga Islands, making repairs after the Battle of the Coral Sea. Vice Admiral William F. Halsey, whose Task Force 16 was made up of the fast carriers *Enterprise* and *Hornet* and their escorts, was steaming off the Solomon Islands. Halsey and his carriers had arrived in the Coral Sea too late to join the battle. Both commanders hastily headed for Pearl Harbor when Nimitz radioed that they were needed there. Halsey's answer had consisted of two brief words: "EXPEDITE RETURN."

Since only makeshift repairs had been made on *Yorktown* at Tongatabu, she was not ready for another major battle. *Yorktown*'s engineers estimated that they would need 90 days in drydock to repair all the damage done at Coral Sea, but the Japanese attack was less than eight days away when the big carrier entered the channel at Pearl Harbor on 27 May. Nimitz ordered the repairs completed in three days.

While yard workers and members of *Yorktown*'s crew worked around the clock to correct the damage done by the 1,000-pound bomb that had hit the carrier, Admiral Nimitz briefed Admiral Fletcher on the Japanese plan. He also ordered Rear Admiral Raymond A. Spruance, a non-aviator, to take command of Task Force 16 when Admiral Halsey had to be hospitalized because of an irritating skin disease. By midday on 30 May, both task forces were back at sea heading independently for a rendezvous northeast of Midway. Their orders from Nimitz were explicit: "Inflict maximum damage on enemy by deploying strong attrition tactics [i.e., air strikes]." Fletcher, as the senior admiral, was in tactical command once the two forces had made their rendezvous; yet Spruance, who had inherited Halsey's aviation staff, was able to exercise command with great latitude during the battle.

Task Forces 16 and 17 were outgunned by the Japanese. The Nagumo Force alone had 2 battleships, 2 heavy cruisers, 1 light cruiser, 11 destroyers and the 4 big carriers, not to mention the 7 battleships and other big warships in Yamamoto's main body, which was steaming eastward some 600 miles astern of the Nagumo Force. Collectively, Fletcher and Spruance had only 3 carriers, 7 heavy cruisers, 1 light cruiser, 14 destroyers and no battleships at all. Nor were the American aviators prepared for battle. *Yorktown*'s new air group was made up mostly of replacement units from the carrier *Saratoga*, which had been torpedoed in January. In the squadrons that were not from *Saratoga*, there was a mix of experienced and inexperienced pilots. The *Enterprise* air group probably had more combat-experienced pilots than either *Yorktown* or *Hornet*, because *Hornet*'s aviators had gotten very little flying in after the Doolittle raid. Ensign George H. Gay of *Hornet*'s Torpedo Squadron Eight summed up to Commander Richard C. Knott the problem of readiness in his squadron in this way:

"Nobody had any experience with [torpedoes]. [Lieutenant Commander John C. Waldron, the squadron skipper] and a couple of Chief NAPs [enlisted pilots] had been in the Navy long enough to know what a torpedo was, but I really didn't know exactly what they looked like until I got out on the ship.

The day I took off with the torpedo [at Midway], I had never seen it done before, much less done it myself—that is, take a torpedo off a carrier. We didn't have any dummies to practice with."

Smoke pours from Midway installations

No wonder the Japanese were overconfident. Even if Ensign Gay's experience was unusual and his comments on torpedo bombing were exaggerated, the Japanese still had reason to believe that they were ready with seasoned pilots, superior aircraft and ships, and the element of surprise to take on the Americans at Midway.

Because Nimitz's intelligence personnel were able to read the Japanese code, they effectively took away any element of surprise the Japanese may have had. Denial of surprise to the enemy gave it, in turn, to the Americans because Nimitz could ignore the Japanese feint in the Aleutians and position his carrier forces so that they could most effectively counter the Nagumo Force.

As planned, the Japanese bombed Dutch Harbor in the Aleutians on 3 and 4 June and followed this up with landings at undefended Attu and Kiska in the western Aleutians. Although there was an American naval force in the area that knew of the Japanese plans, it was not able to prevent the occupation of American territory in Alaska.

Meanwhile, the Nagumo Force approached Midway under heavy clouds and fog. Although PBY Catalina patrol planes flew out of Midway on daily search missions, they were unable to locate the First Carrier Striking Force in the overcast weather. Nevertheless a Catalina did spot the Midway occupation force to the southwest of the island on 3 June. The Midway defenders struck back first with Army B-17s and then with Navy PBYs. Between them, the two attacks in the early hours of 4 June managed only one hit.

When Admiral Nimitz received notice that the Japanese transport group had been located and attacked, he sent word to Admiral Fletcher that this initial contact was not the carrier striking force. As dawn broke on 4 June, Nagumo and his carriers were on a southeasterly course approaching the launch point about 230 miles from Midway. The evening before, Fletcher and his carriers had changed course to a southwesterly heading so that they would be in a position to launch their strikes on the Japanese flank once the enemy carriers had been located the next morning.

The night of 3 June was one of work, worry and wait for both sides. Last-minute details were gone over, double and triple checks were made on aircraft, and final instructions issued. For example, as Walter Lord reports in *Incredible Victory*, Lieutenant Commander Waldron, skipper of Torpedo Squadron 8 on *Hornet*, told his men that he felt they were all ready for the battle. Then he added:

"We have had a very short time to train and we have worked under the most severe difficulties. But we have truly done the best humanly possible. I actually believe that under these conditions we are the best in the world. My greatest hope is that we encounter a favorable tactical situation, but if we don't, and the worst comes to worst, I want each of you to do his utmost to destroy our enemies. If there is only one plane left to make a final run in, I want that man to go in and get a hit. May God be with us all. Good luck, happy landings and give 'em hell."

On *Enterprise* the situation was not much different. Lieutenant Jim Gray, commander of Fighting Six on that carrier, put his feelings into one succinct sentence: "It is doubtful that there were any atheists in *Enterprise* on the night of 3 June 1942."

For the Japanese the situation was remarkably similar. Commander Takashi Kanoe purposefully stopped at the ship's shrine on the carrier *Hiryu* while he was en route to the bridge that evening. When Captain Fuchida became ill with appendicitis, Lieutenant Joichi Tomonaga was chosen to replace him as leader of the Midway attack group. Commander Genda was also sick, but he and Fuchida both managed to pull themselves up to the bridge for the launch at about 4:30 A.M. Once in the air and formed up, the strike group totalled 36 high-level bombers from *Hiryu* and *Soryu;* 36 dive-bombers from *Kaga* and *Akagi;* and 36 fighters, 9 from each of the carriers. They headed for Midway, some 200 miles to the southeast.

Once the attackers had gone, the carrier deck crews began to arm their second strike force. Because Nagumo worried about American surface forces, the ordnancemen mounted torpedoes on 36 high-level bombers, armor-piercing missiles on 36 dive-bombers, and the usual machine gun and 20-mm shells on the 36 Zero fighters. Once armed, the planes were brought on deck ready for launching on short notice. At the same time as the ordnancemen were arming the planes of the second strike force, the escorting cruisers were launching search planes that would sweep out 300 miles to the east over an arc of 165°, just to make sure that there were no American carriers around. These floatplanes were scheduled to depart at 4:30, but the last of them, one from the cruiser *Tone*, was a half hour late getting off due to catapult trouble.

A few minutes after 6:00 A.M. on 4 June, Admiral Fletcher got a message that had just come in from one of the PBYs flying out of Midway: "MANY PLANES HEADING MIDWAY, BEARING 320, DISTANCE 150." This report was followed by others that identified two carriers and escorts all steaming on course 135° at 25 knots. Fletcher gave his orders to Spruance: "Proceed southwesterly and attack enemy carriers when definitely located. Will follow as soon as search planes recovered."

By 6:30 the Japanese planes were over Midway, dropping their bombs and strafing the island. The defenders put up a voluminous antiaircraft fire. Tomonaga, for one, took a hit which drained the gas tank in his left wing. As leader of the strike, Tomonaga knew that the Americans on Midway had been ready. They had got their planes in the air and had put up a spirited defensive fire. Damage had been done to Midway installations, but not enough, especially to the aircraft. Tomonaga therefore radioed back to Nagumo: THERE IS NEED FOR A SECOND ATTACK.

With no sign of the American fleet, Nagumo and his staff could confidently send their reserve air strength to Midway to carry out its neutralization as planned. But they were still worried that the Americans might be in the area. The problem that Nagumo had to weigh was aggravated by air attacks on his force by planes from Midway. In four waves the Americans swarmed over the carriers. B-17s, B-26s, Navy TBF Avengers, SBDs and TBD Devastators all tried to get at the carriers, but the fighters and the adroit maneuvering of the ships kept them from being damaged by bombs or torpedoes.

In the midst of these attacks Nagumo received word that the floatplane from the cruiser *Tone* had sighted an enemy surface force of 10 ships within striking range of the Japanese carriers. The problem was now compounded. Because Tomonaga had called for a second strike, the reserve aircraft had been taken below decks to be rearmed with bombs. Should Nagumo go after Midway or should he strike out immediately at the enemy ships even if there were no carriers with them? The admiral ordered the search plane from *Tone* to provide more details.

The answer at 8:09 was no carriers, only cruisers and destroyers. In the meantime, more fighters had been launched to protect the Nagumo Force against these insistent, but relatively futile, attacks from Midway. Tomonaga and his fliers arrived over their carriers just as the fourth Midway attack was ending. The Japanese carriers were untouched by enemy bombs or torpedoes, but *Tone*'s search plane now radioed that there was an American carrier out there and a fifth Midway group began its attack to complicate Nagumo's problems.

Some planes on deck in the second Japanese attack group had land bombs; the others were below decks because they were to be armed with torpedoes. Tomonaga's planes were low on fuel and wanted to land. What should Nagumo do—launch everything he had immediately, regardless of weaponry, or recover his planes, arm them properly, and then hit the Americans?

Nagumo conferred with his staff. Commander Genda recommended recovering the first attack group and the fighters, rearming and refueling them, and then hitting the enemy force. Once again the flight deck crews and ordnancemen had to change weapons. This time torpedoes and armor-piercing bombs were required. Because of the lack of time, the land bombs were simply rolled out of the way on deck and not returned to the magazines. At 8:37 Tomonaga's planes began to land; 11 planes hadn't made it back.

Once all the Japanese planes had been recovered, Nagumo changed course to the northeast, a direction that would aid their attack on the enemy surface force. Just when the strike force commander and his staff thought all was beginning to shape up as they expected, a new threat, 15 American torpedo planes, was sighted. This was John Waldron's Torpedo Squadron 8 from *Hornet*.

Ensign Gay, the lone survivor of Torpedo Eight's subsequent suicidal charge on the Japanese carriers, described what the attack was like:

> The Japanese combat air patrol was waiting for us at altitude—about 75 Zeros. Since we were the first to get there, we sucked them all down. Why they *all* came down with the experience they had, I don't know. I guess it was overconfidence and it was a fatal mistake, because when our dive bombers showed up a few minutes later they had no opposition.
>
> . . . The next thing we knew there were Zeros swarming all over us. They started knocking off our planes just like that! [Snapping his fingers several times in rapid succession.] I saw them all go in the water except one. We were wiped out on the way in. I was the only one who got in close enough to make an attack.

Miraculously, Ensign Gay survived the attack by the Zeros and made his way into the Japanese antiaircraft fire, where the enemy fighters refused to follow him. Although he managed to launch his torpedo, probably at the carrier *Kaga*, it missed.

Since the safest way out was straight ahead, Gay "bore-sighted" the carrier and flew down its flight deck. "I saw the captain on the bridge waving his binoculars and I went out the stern and flew past a couple of big cruisers. Everybody was shooting at me—the whole fleet." Eventually the Zeros got him when he came out of the antiaircraft fire on the other side, but although he was wounded, Gay managed to escape his sinking plane and spent the remainder of the day in the water, where he had a "fish-eye view" of the action. The next day, 5 June, a U.S. PBY patrol plane spotted Ensign Gay in his life raft and rescued him after 30 hours in the water.

Courageous as the attack of Torpedo Eight was, it caused no damage to enemy carriers. Neither did the torpedo squadron from *Enterprise* which followed up the attack of Waldron's squadron. *Enterprise*'s Torpedo Squadron 6 lost 10 out of 14 aircraft and the next attack, from *Yorktown*'s Torpedo Three, lost 9 out of 13 Devastators. These ancient aircraft, no match for the Zeros, were ill equipped to attack the carriers and their powerful escorts. Of the 42 Devastators that attacked, none scored a hit that day.

Just when Nagumo and his men could begin to think that Midway would soon be theirs, the tide of battle reversed itself. At 10:26 *Enterprise*'s Dauntless dive-bombers found the enemy carriers. The air group

SBDs begin a dive-bombing run

commander, Lieutenant Commander Clarence W. McClusky, divided his 37 planes into two groups which took off after *Kaga* and *Akagi*. Since the Zeros were all down low on the water from chasing the torpedo bombers, there was almost no opposition to the SBDs when they hurtled down from 14,000 feet.

As the *Enterprise* SBDs dove on their targets, they could see that there were other Dauntlesses on the attack as well. These were SBDs from Bombing Squadron 3 on *Yorktown*, led by Lieutenant Commander Maxwell F. Leslie. These 13 planes were after the 18,000-ton *Soryu*.

The results of these three attacks were incredible. Lieutenant Clarence E. Dickinson, in one of the SBDs from *Enterprise*, described his

Lieutenant Commander
Clarence W. McClusky

carrier target as "utterly satisfying." As he made his approach, he saw the bombs of those attacking ahead of him straddle *Kaga* so that they "grabbed at her like an ice man's tongs." After another bomb hit the carrier, he "saw the deck rippling, and curling back in all directions exposing a great section of the hangar below." Then he dropped his own bombs. "I saw the 500-pound bomb hit right abreast of the island. The two 100-pound bombs struck in the forward area of the parked planes on that yellow flight deck. Then I began thinking it was time to get myself away from there and try to get back alive."

Fighting off Zeros and dodging antiaircraft fire, Dickinson and his tail gunner did get away alive. When he had flown several miles from the *Kaga*, he looked back at the scene he had just left:

> ". . . the three biggest fires were the carriers. They were burning fiercely and exploding . . . [*Kaga*] was on fire from end to end and I saw her blow up at the middle. From right abreast the island a ball of solid fire shot straight up. It passed through the fleecy lower clouds which we estimated to be 1200 feet above the water . . . Probably that was gasoline but many of the explosions I was seeing in those three carriers were, I think, from their own bombs parked below on the hangar decks in readiness for planes to be rearmed."

Although Dickinson was talking specifically about *Kaga,* the situation was similar on *Akagi* and *Soryu. Akagi* had taken a bomb on her hangar deck that exploded gasoline and ordnance. Subsequently, Admiral Nagumo had to abandon his flagship for a cruiser. *Akagi* was then sunk by torpedoes from a Japanese destroyer. *Kaga* took four bomb hits just as Dickinson described them. She sank from the results of internal explosions. *Soryu* took three 1,000-pound bomb hits and also had to be abandoned. The U.S. submarine *Nautilus* then dispatched *Soryu* with three torpedoes that broke the carrier in two.

Even though the Japanese had lost three fast carriers within the space of about 10 minutes, they were not finished. Nagumo ordered the undamaged *Hiryu* to strike *Yorktown,* which the cruiser's search planes had located. By following returning aircraft back in the general direction of the American carriers, 18 dive-bombers, 10 torpedo bombers and 12 fighters were able to attack *Yorktown.*

Lieutenant Commander John S. Thach, skipper of *Yorktown*'s Fighter Squadron 3, described what happened:

> "Fourteen of the bombers were shot down but four got through, and that was enough. A few more planes on our side would have got them. The four that got through dropped their bombs—with three hits out of four. One was very lucky; it went down the smokestack into the machinery spaces and stopped the ship. We were dead in the water."

Another bomb went through the ship's stack and exploded on the flight deck, blowing a huge hole in the middle of it. The third bomb set a fire that killed a gun crew and wounded others on the flight deck.

Meanwhile, Thach and his fighters were doing everything to drive off or spoil the Japanese attack. While Thach was shooting down an enemy torpedo plane, a Zero got on his tail. "The first I knew about it was the stream of tracer bullets which looked like red rain coming past both my ears. I rolled and pulled hard to the side and the Zero slipped past."

With *Yorktown* crippled, Admiral Fletcher transferred his flag to the cruiser *Astoria.* Then planes from *Hiryu* were back for a second attack. This time they were less successful, but two torpedoes caught the big carrier on her port side. The explosions and damage done by these hits undid all the repair efforts that had been made after the first attack. Soon *Yorktown* had a 26° list. Since power was gone, counterflooding was impossible. Unable to stop the flooding below decks, *Yorktown*'s captain gave the order to abandon ship.

While *Yorktown* was battling for her life, the Japanese carrier *Hiryu*

Yorktown is battered by a series of bombs

Yorktown loses the battle for life

Japanese heavy cruiser after attack by U.S. dive-bombers

was also trying to stave off air attacks. About 5:00 P.M. 14 SBDs from *Enterprise* and 10 from *Yorktown* found the last enemy flattop. She took four bomb hits which put her out of commission. *Hiryu* eventually sank in the early hours of the morning of 5 June.

Following the successful attack on *Hiryu*, Admiral Spruance ordered the undamaged American forces to withdraw eastward during the night. They later headed back to the west, catching the remnants of the Japanese forces, and sank one cruiser and damaged another. By that time, however, the Battle of Midway was effectively over. When he received the news of the loss of four carriers, Admiral Yamamoto ordered his surviving forces to withdraw. The only consolation the Japanese could wring from the battle

65

was the damage to *Yorktown* and her eventual loss when the submarine *I-168* put two torpedoes into her and a third into a destroyer that was assisting in salvage operations after the battle.

The Japanese losses were staggering. Yamamoto had lost his entire carrier group, some 250 aircraft, the majority of their pilots and about 2,200 officers and men. The Japanese would never be able to replace the carriers or the pilots during the remainder of the war. In contrast, the United States lost the carrier *Yorktown*, the destroyer *Hammann*, 150 aircraft and 307 officers and men.

Although greatly outgunned by the Japanese, Admirals Fletcher and Spruance had convincingly demonstrated that naval guns were not supreme when carrier air power was involved. Their well-directed thrust with *Hornet, Yorktown* and *Enterprise* had wrested victory from a numerically superior foe.

News of the victory at Midway was quickly spread by the newspapers in the United States, but in Japan the military leadership announced that they too had achieved a great victory, although at some loss (a carrier, a cruiser and 35 planes). The reality was, of course, somewhat different. Captain Fuchida, who was injured in the battle, got a painful taste of the "extreme measures taken to preserve secrecy" about what really happened when he was returned to Japan. Taken to a hospital on a covered stretcher at night, he was carried in through the rear entrance. His room was completely isolated, and he was not allowed to communicate with the outside world. In short, he wrote, "it was really confinement in the guise of medical treatment, and I sometimes had the feeling of being a prisoner of war."

5. Stalemate

In his book about carrier operations in World War II, Admiral Frederick C. Sherman designated the period of time between the Battle of Midway and November 1943, when the Allies took Tarawa in the Gilbert Islands, a time of stalemate. The admiral's point is that in the 17 months from Midway to Tarawa, although there were some important battles, primarily in the Southwest Pacific around Guadalcanal, neither side was able to obtain more than temporary control of the air or the sea. Sherman's opinion has support from Admiral King's official report on the course of the war, in which the observation is made that this period was one of "offensive-defensive" action.

Stalemate or offensive-defensive combat may characterize carrier operations in this year and a half, but these labels omit a very important part of what was going on for the carrier forces of both fleets. In the wake of their defeat at Midway, the Japanese proceeded to reorganize and consolidate their remaining carrier forces so that they were subsequently able to inflict substantial losses on the Americans in the Battle of Santa Cruz. The U.S. Navy was also busy, primarily with building new carriers and naval aircraft that would provide the weapons necessary to take the offensive against Japan.

Although Japan had lost a total of five carriers at the Coral Sea and Midway in contrast to two for the U.S. Navy, she still had the powerful *Zuikaku* and *Shokaku* in reserve. In addition, she could deploy the fast carriers *Hosho, Ryuho, Amagi, Junyo* and *Taiho* and a number of light carriers. Significantly, the Naval General Staff also ordered the third *Yamato*-class battleship, *Shinano*, converted to an aircraft carrier. Once finished, *Shinano* would be the largest carrier afloat at 68,060 tons.

The carrier forces of the United States in the latter half of 1942 were hardly impressive. With the loss of *Lexington* and *Yorktown*, the U.S. Navy had only *Saratoga, Enterprise, Hornet* and *Wasp* in the Pacific. Nevertheless, by late 1942 the industrial capacity of the United States was beginning to give the Americans the edge in the race to rebuild the carrier fleets. While the Japanese were completing work on carriers already

laid down, or converting merchantmen and battleships to carriers or even beginning new construction, the Americans were undertaking a vastly more ambitious program.

The carrier construction program in the United States simultaneously headed in four parallel directions. Existing carriers were improved with advanced radar, greater torpedo protection, new aircraft and more antiaircraft guns. Second, the Navy converted nine light cruiser hulls to light carriers (10,000 tons). Third, it either built new escort carriers (also called "jeep" carriers) or converted merchant hulls to jeep carriers. Last, it began building new fast carriers of the *Essex* class (27,000 tons) and the even larger *Midway* class (45,000 tons) to augment the existing fast carrier force. Thus by the end of 1942 the U.S. Navy had five *Essex*-class carriers under construction and another six on order. As the carrier building program gained momentum after Midway, the United States commissioned nine fast carriers alone between 31 December 1942 and mid-June 1943. This total was

New USS *Lexington* replaces the famous "Lady Lex"

one more carrier than the Navy had had when the Japanese attacked Pearl Harbor. By the time of the Japanese surrender in 1945, the U.S. Navy had a total of 28 fast carriers in commissioned service.

In sheer numbers, the program for building escort carriers was even more staggering than the fast carrier construction project. By July 1942 the U.S. Navy had a total of 99 escort carriers in various stages of construction, conversion or on order. Thirty-four of these vessels ultimately went to the Royal Navy, which played a significant role in the development of the aircraft carrier both before and during World War II.

When the war broke out in Europe in September 1939, the Royal Navy at first used its carriers to hunt German U-boats. However, in mid-September the *U-29* torpedoed the carrier *Courageous*, taking 1,779 lives, a loss that forced the British Admiralty to withdraw its carriers from antisubmarine operations because of their vulnerability.

The fleet carrier *Ark Royal* subsequently distinguished herself in operations against the German pocket battleship *Graf Spee* and with the carrier *Victorious* in sinking the famous dreadnought *Bismarck*. But the U-boats got *Ark Royal*, too. In November 1941 she and another carrier, *Argus*, were engaged in Operation Perpetual, a mission to ferry aircraft from the British base at Gibraltar to the island of Malta in the middle of the Mediterranean. After they had delivered their planes to Malta, *Ark Royal* was hit by a single torpedo from *U-81*. At first the great carrier did not seem mortally wounded by the torpedo hit, but counterflooding and efforts to repair the damage were not enough. An eyewitness, Rear Admiral Sir William Jameson, subsequently described the scene after *Ark Royal* went down:

> When the sun came up there was nothing left except a great patch of oil and some floating debris. The sea was so absolutely calm that rats, which successive first lieutenants had tried vainly to dislodge, could be seen swimming around, each one leaving a little "V" as it parted the water. A careful check accounted for all but one of her [*Ark Royal*'s] company. . . . An ML [motor launch] nosing amongst the debris found one of the ship's cats clinging to a piece of wood, angry but quite unharmed. Sadly the tugs and escorts headed for home. There was quite a concourse of ships west of Gibraltar, but the sea looked strangely bare. Patrolling flying-boats had gone, and the sky was quite empty.

Because British carriers were frequently engaged in convoy operations or ferrying aircraft to places like Malta, they did not have many opportunities to take the offensive in the manner of Japanese or American carriers. The new fast carrier *Illustrious*, which had an armored flight deck and radar, did, however, carry out a daring raid on the Italian fleet anchored at the port of Taranto.

Twenty-one Swordfish fighters from *Illustrious* hit Taranto on 11 November 1940 with bombs and torpedoes. Lieutenant M. R. Maund of 824 Squadron of the Fleet Air Arm (the British designation for naval aviation) was one of those who participated in the attack. After leaving the carrier and finding the harbor, Maund encountered heavy antiaircraft fire. He felt it was "as though all hell comes tumbling in on top of us . . . leaving only two things in my mind, the line of approach to the dropping position and a wild desire to escape the effects of this deathly hailstorm." He made his approach take him down as close to the water as possible. "The water is close beneath our wheels, so close I'm wondering which is to happen first—the torpedo going or our hitting the sea—then we level out, and almost without thought the button is pressed and a jerk tells me the 'fish' is gone."

Maund and his colleagues hit the Italian warships hard, sinking one battleship, badly damaging two more, and doing additional damage to a cruiser and destroyer. Despite the intense antiaircraft fire, the British raiders lost only two aircraft. Although the damage done in this attack put the Italian Navy permanently on the defensive, the raid had an importance beyond the balance of forces in the Mediterranean, because Admiral Yamamoto and others in Japan studied it in detail while they were planning the attack on Pearl Harbor. Perhaps the Americans should have paid more attention to it, too.

Illustrious soon suffered heavily for the raid on Taranto. The Germans sent their Fliegerkorps X to the aid of their Italian allies. This X Air Corps flew gull-winged monoplane dive-bombers, the Ju 87 Stuka, and they caught *Illustrious* off Pantellaria on 10 January 1941. Kenneth Poolman, a newspaper correspondent aboard the carrier, described one of their attacks:

High-level bombers came over this time as well [as the Stukas]. Once again the ship lurched and staggered as bombs fell all around her. Noise between decks was terrifying, like a thousand Tube trains roaring out of a tunnel. A bomb smashed through the flight-deck and through the boys' mess deck. Passing out of the ship's side it hit the water and exploded. White-hot metal shot in all directions, holing the ship in many places above and below the waterline and causing bad flooding in the unarmoured for'ard section. Blast from the same bomb smashed aircraft in the hangar and punched the for'ard lift [elevator] upwards into an arch. Wind rushed immediately into the hangar through this arch, and fanned the fires there into a great blaze.

Illustrious, however, was a tough ship. Despite six direct hits, she somehow managed to stay afloat and retreat to Malta, where she underwent emergency repairs while still under attack. Later, after she had

Off North Africa USS *Ranger* launches an F4F

been repaired, *Illustrious* slipped out of the Mediterranean through the Suez Canal.

The fight to keep Malta alive continued. Because of her strategic position in the midst of the Mediterranean, Malta was an ideal air base for keeping track of enemy ship movements and for disrupting the flow of supplies from the Italian mainland to Axis forces operating in North Africa. In April 1942 the United States loaned the carrier *Wasp* to the British so that she could help ferry Spitfire fighters to Malta.

In August 1942 the British War Cabinet ordered another convoy to ferry fighters and supplies to the beleaguered Malta. The force that left Gibraltar for Operation Pedestal, as the resupply mission was called, consisted of 14 merchant ships, 2 battleships, 7 cruisers, 32 destroyers and 4 carriers (*Victorious, Indomitable, Eagle* and *Furious*).

One carrier pilot, Lieutenant Hugh Popham of 880 Squadron, flew off his carrier on a patrol mission and then returned to the convoy to discover that he could not come in to land because the ships in the convoy were firing at anything that flew. When he got down to 10 gallons of fuel, Popham prepared to ditch his plane in the sea. He later wrote:

"I . . . began to go over in my mind the procedure for ditching, for if I wasn't shot down, and I didn't find a deck to land on very soon, I should surely have to land in the sea. I jettisoned the hood and released my parachute harness and kept ducking the gusts of gun-fire, and came, all at once, to the sudden stabbing realization that this might be the end of me. . . . Now it hit me, as blindly bruising as hatred, as confusing as a blow. I didn't know how I was going to get back aboard: now, for the first time, it seemed highly probable that I should not, and I understood the implications."

Fighting the antiaircraft fire all the way down, Popham found the friendly deck of *Victorious*, where he crash-landed his Sea Hurricane which "went up in a haze of flame" just after he had scrambled out of the cockpit. Operation Pedestal got through to Malta, but not without damage. The convoy lost nine merchant ships, two cruisers, a destroyer and the carrier *Eagle* en route. *Indomitable* was also damaged by three bomb hits.

Despite all the efforts of the Germans and Italians to cut off Malta, the British were able to keep planes and supplies coming into the island. Between 1940 and 1942, the Royal Navy ferried 718 single-engine aircraft and a number of merchant ships to this outpost in the middle of the Mediterranean in a total of 25 trips. Malta endured frequent attacks on its line of supply until November 1942, when the Allies invaded North Africa and thereby shifted Axis attention to a more immediate threat.

British convoys such as the one in Operation Pedestal had to be alert to attacks from both enemy aircraft and submarines. Thus from the early days of the war in Europe, the British experimented with ways to take aircraft to sea with their merchant convoys. Initially, they mounted a catapult on the bow of a merchant ship so that a single Sea Hurricane fighter could be launched against a German U-boat or reconnaissance plane. This system of Catapult Armed Merchant (CAM) ships was very limited, how-

Ill-fated carrier *Block Island* catapults an F6F

ever, because the pilot had either to fly to a shore base or to parachute into the sea.

The CAM ship was the first step toward the development of the escort carrier. Then in June 1941 the Admiralty converted a German merchant prize into a carrier with a flight deck 475 feet long. HMS *Audacity*, as she was renamed, carried six Grumman F4F-3 Wildcat fighters (renamed Martlets by the British) at a maximum speed of 15 knots. Since *Audacity* had no hangar, the Martlets were parked on her flight deck when not on patrol over the convoy. During convoy runs between Gibraltar and England in September and October 1941, *Audacity* kept two fighters in the air over her merchant charges and two more at the ready to drive off any menacing U-boats. In December she proved just how effective an escort carrier could be in providing fighter and antisubmarine protection when she shepherded 30 merchant ships from Gibraltar to England through a four-day running battle with a German wolfpack. Although the U-boats were not able to sink any of the merchant ships, *U-75* was able to torpedo *Audacity* and another U-boat sank a destroyer. German losses were heavy: five U-boats sunk and two reconnaissance planes shot down.

Nearly 15 months passed before the United States could build enough escort carriers for them to have any real impact on the war against the submarine. In the meantime, the British converted 19 grain or tanker hulls to escort carriers called Merchant Aircraft Carriers (MAC ships). Each MAC ship carried four Swordfish fighters, but like the CAM ships they had very limited operational capabilities.

In March 1943 the first escort carriers (CVEs) built in the United States joined the Battle of the Atlantic. They served as escorts for merchant convoys crossing the Atlantic or Mediterranean or operating as part of Hunter-Killer Groups (HUK groups) in search of U-boats. Their aircraft were either Grumman TBF Avenger torpedo bombers or Grumman F4F Wildcat fighters, which operated in conjunction with a half-dozen destroyers. Smaller and slower than fast carriers, the escort carriers usually had an air group consisting of 30 fighters and torpedo bombers.

In the Atlantic, the escort carriers were very effective. They not only prevented the U-boats from sinking merchantmen, they also sank a total of 33 U-boats and shared credit for sinking 12 others between April 1943 and September 1944. Two escort carriers, USS *Bogue* and USS *Card*, each sank eight enemy submarines with their aircraft. The U-boats obtained some small revenge for their losses in the last two and a half years of the war when *U-549* put three torpedoes into the escort carrier *Block Island* on 29 May 1944. In contrast, Captain Dan Gallery's CVE *Guadalcanal* managed a rare feat when it assisted in the boarding and capture of *U-505* in early June 1944.

Escort carriers served in another important capacity in the Atlantic and Mediterranean besides antisubmarine operations. They proved to be nearly indispensable in amphibious landing operations. The CVEs provided air cover for the landings in North Africa (November 1942), Sicily (10 July 1943), the Italian mainland at Salerno (3 September 1943) and D-Day at Normandy (6 June 1944). During each of these amphibious assaults (except for Normandy), air patrols from the escort carriers provided antisubmarine protection and close air support for troops ashore.

Paralleling the development of the escort carrier for convoy and antisubmarine operations were the efforts of aircraft designers and manufacturers in the United States to build planes that could outperform the vaunted Japanese Mitsubishi Zero (also called "Zeke"). Introduced to combat in China in August 1940, the Zero in its later standard production model—the A6M5 Model 52—had a maximum speed of 351 miles per hour, a 19,700-foot ceiling and great maneuverability. Its armament consisted of fixed .50-caliber machine guns in the wings and twin 20-mm cannon. In contrast, the Grumman F4F-3 Wildcat fighter of the U.S. Navy had a maximum speed of 331 miles per hour at 21,300 feet with a ceiling of 37,000 feet. Armament on the Wildcat consisted of four .50-caliber machine guns and two 100-pound bombs.

As the Battle of Midway demonstrated, the U.S. Navy needed planes that could perform with the Zero in combat. The pilots and crew members who flew the Douglas TBD Devastators against the Nagumo Force, for ex-

USS *Guadalcanal* and the captured *U-505*

TBF Avenger, the largest U.S. carrier
plane of the war

ample, had flown what amounted to suicidal missions. These torpedo planes had become operational in 1935 and were effectively obsolete by 1942. The Devastator had a maximum speed of only 206 miles per hour at 8,000 feet and a ceiling of 19,700 feet. It was extremely vulnerable to fighter attack, especially because of its slow rate of climb after the pilot had released his torpedo.

The Devastator saw its last major action at Midway as it was being phased out. In that battle the Grumman TBF Avenger got its first combat test. The largest American carrier aircraft in World War II, the Avenger had a maximum speed of 271 miles per hour, carried a torpedo or a 2,000-pound bomb, and was flown by a three-man crew of pilot, gunner and bombardier-radioman.

Until 1943 the U.S. carrier fleet's principal dive-bomber and scouting aircraft was the Douglas SBD Dauntless. The SBD-3 had a maximum speed of 250 miles per hour at 16,000 feet with a ceiling of 27,100 feet. The pilot operated two forward-firing .50-caliber wing machine guns and his radioman-gunner could operate a pair of flexible .30-caliber machine guns aft. The SBD carried either a 500-pound or a 1,000-pound bomb.

Versatile as the SBD was, it lacked range, speed and bombload. To attain these, Curtiss-Wright had for some time been developing a new dive-bomber, the SB2C Helldiver, which underwent its first carrier trials in the spring of 1943. Although there were many problems with this new plane, an improved Helldiver joined the carrier fleet in the fall of 1943. Its payload could be either a torpedo or 2,650 pounds of bombs, and its maximum speed (for the SB2C-3) was 294 miles per hour at 16,700 feet.

When the Helldiver became operational in the fall of 1943, the technological battle between aircraft designers was still being fought. Masatake Okumiya, a Japanese aviator, and Jiro Horikoshi, an aeronautical engineer, have written that the Zero fighter was the "symbol not only of our land- and sea-based air power but of the entire Japanese military force." The Helldiver was one of the planes that could match the Zero; the others were the Chance-Vought F4U Corsair and the Grumman F6F Hellcat.

The development of the Corsair and the Hellcat got an unexpected assist from the Japanese following the attack on the Aleutians in the Midway campaign. When one of the fighter pilots taking part in the Aleutian operations was forced to make an emergency landing on an island east of Dutch Harbor, his wheels stuck in the soft tundra, tipping his Zero over and killing him. The American forces in the area subsequently discovered the plane, removed it intact to the United States, and then subjected it to exhaustive flight tests. These tests revealed that the Zero had unusually light weight which contributed to its high performance, and that it had cer-

SB2C Helldivers

tain weaknesses: poor diving qualities, limited ceiling and lack of armor protection.

Development of the Chance-Vought Corsair had begun in 1938, but it did not make its combat debut until early 1943. Like the Helldiver, it had problems in the beginning when it was first tried as a carrier plane. Carrier tests showed it had poor deck-landing characteristics. Yet the Corsair soon won a place with the U.S. Marines as a land-based fighter. With a maximum speed of 417 miles per hour at 19,900 feet (36,900-foot ceiling), this inverted gull-winged fighter could handle the Zero. By the end of the war, it had established an 11.3:1 kill-to-loss ratio in air-to-air combat with Japanese planes.

The greater beneficiary of the capture of the Zero in the Aleutians was the Grumman F6F-3 Hellcat. Its maximum speed of 376 miles per hour at 22,000 feet established it as a fighter superior to the Zero. As the standard fighter of the fast carriers from 1943 on, the Hellcat was well armored, had six .50-caliber machine guns and could carry two 1,000-pound bombs or rockets. It established the unbelievable kill-to-loss ratio in aerial combat with the Japanese of 19:1.

With the arrival of the Helldiver, the Corsair and the Hellcat in 1943, the air combat situation between the United States and Japan began to change in the favor of the Americans. Okumiya and Horikoshi, summing up that changing situation from the Japanese perspective say that

> early in the war and, in fact, until the later stages of the Guadalcanal battle [late 1942–early 1943], the Zero clearly demonstrated its superior performance over enemy fighter planes. The Americans, however, bent every effort to augment and replace their inferior fighters with new planes of outstanding performance, and soon the Zero met increasing numbers of remarkably fast and powerful enemy fighters. In the interim we were forced to retain the Zero as our frontline fighter; the Navy did not have a suitable successor to the Zero, nor did the Army have an airplane which could favorably contest the American planes.

Besides being outstripped technologically in carriers and aircraft, Japan had also lost ground with respect to pilots and their training by mid-1943. Pilot losses at Coral Sea and Midway began to have serious consequences. In early 1942 Japanese carrier pilots were an elite group of aviators. They averaged 700 hours of flight time in training. Their counterparts in the U.S. Navy at that time averaged only about 305 hours of flight time. By mid-1943, however, attrition had begun to take its toll in the Japanese training programs. While the U.S. Navy was training thousands of new pilots at Pensacola, Jacksonville and Corpus Christi, the Japanese had lost

F4Us in formation

more experienced men than they could replace effectively. The Japanese pilot of mid-1943 averaged only 500 hours of flight training, while the American pilots had increased their average air training time from 305 hours to the same 500 hours.

Given all these changes in carrier development, aircraft and pilot training, the period of stalemate in carrier operations in the Pacific between June 1942 and November 1943 was hardly surprising. For the Japanese it was a time of reorganization and adjustment to the defensive. For the United States it was a time of changing from the defensive to the limited offensive. The growing presence of the new *Essex*-class carriers, the escort carriers and aircraft such as the Avenger, Helldiver, Corsair and Hellcat forced a period of experimentation and trial-and-error on the fast carrier forces of the U.S. Navy. The first real test of the multiple fast carrier task force would not come until Operation Galvanic in the Gilbert Islands in November 1943, but in the meantime, the American fast carriers gained valuable experience in the Southwest Pacific when they assisted in the landings at Guadalcanal.

6. The Bloody Brawling For Guadalcanal

Following the victory at Midway, General Douglas MacArthur, Supreme Commander of the Southwest Pacific Area, informed his superiors in Washington that the situation was ripe for a full-scale assault on the Japanese holdings in New Britain and New Ireland. Success there could lead to seizure of the major Japanese base at Rabaul and control of the Bismarck Sea area. The first step in this offensive would have to be an amphibious assault on Tulagi and Guadalcanal, particularly the latter, because intelligence reports indicated that the Japanese were building an airstrip on the island.

Under the direction of the Joint Chiefs of Staff, Admiral Nimitz mustered what naval forces he could to assist in the operation, code-named Watchtower. Overall naval command was given to Vice Admiral Robert L. Ghormley, but the commander of the assault forces was Rear Admiral Frank Jack Fletcher. Fletcher would have three carrier groups, organized around *Enterprise*, *Wasp* and *Saratoga*. Rear Admiral Richmond Kelly Turner commanded the amphibious forces, and Major General Alexander A. Vandegrift of the Marine Corps was in command of about 19,000 leathernecks embarked on 19 transports.

The subsequent fighting, indeed brawling, between these American forces and the Japanese defenders of Guadalcanal was important for two reasons. First, the campaign itself involved seven major naval battles (two of which were primarily carrier-versus-carrier engagements), no fewer than 10 land battles and a host of less noteworthy encounters on land and sea. Secondly, Operation Watchtower was the first application of Admiral King's "offensive-defensive" strategy and the first step in the Allied drive toward Tokyo. Thus it provides an instructive look at the emerging air navy of the United States—a force that would fight its way toward the Japanese capital, riding on the shoulders of the American productive system, which would forge the new weapons of war that would be necessary to achieve victory in the Pacific.

In July, Fletcher's Task Force 61 held a brief rehearsal in the Fiji Islands for its amphibious assault, and it then entered the Solomon Sea on 6 August 1942. The next day Vandegrift's marines hit the beaches at Tulagi and Guadalcanal in the first American amphibious assault since 1898. They caught the Japanese by surprise and rapidly gained control of Tulagi and the airstrip on Guadalcanal by evening of 8 August.

Nakajima Kates carrying
torpedoes

Japanese aircraft warm up on a carrier flight deck

Although the Japanese had suffered a grave defeat at Midway, they were by no means out of the war. Their power had been shaken but not destroyed in that battle. Thus they responded rapidly and adroitly to this unexpected American initiative. Fighters and bombers from as far away as Rabaul were ordered to attack the enemy assault force. But the Japanese bombers met with little success, because they tried to hit the U.S. Navy ships by horizontal bombing at 13,000 feet rather than with torpedoes. Flight Petty Officer First Class Saburo Sakai was one of the fighter pilots sent from Rabaul to escort these bombers to Guadalcanal. Soon Sakai was locked in a desperate struggle with the pilot of a carrier-based Grumman Wildcat.

"Neither of us could gain an advantage," he later wrote. "We held to the spiral, tremendous G pressures pushing us down in our seats with every passing second. My heart pounded wildly, and my head felt as if it weighed a ton. A gray film seemed to be clouding over my eyes. I gritted my teeth; if the enemy pilot could take the punishment, so could I. The man who failed first and turned in any other direction to ease the pressure would be finished."

On the sixth spiral, the American made the mistake of trying to loop his Wildcat. The Zero was more maneuverable and cut the distance down inside the loop. Yet when Sakai subsequently pumped 200 rounds of machine gun fire into the Grumman's cockpit, the plane stayed aloft because, unlike the Zero, it had armor protection for the pilot. Finally Sakai set the Wildcat's engine on fire with a blast of cannon fire; the American bailed out.

On the day after Sakai's duel with the American fighter pilot over Guadalcanal, the Japanese inflicted a costly defeat on the U.S. naval forces guarding the assault beaches at Guadalcanal, in a night surface gunnery engagement called the Battle of Savo Island. When the sun rose next morning on the sound that stretched between Tulagi and Guadalcanal, the Allied naval force had lost the Australian cruiser *Canberra* and the American cruisers *Astoria, Vincennes* and *Quincy.* Another cruiser, *Chicago,* was badly damaged and a destroyer was also sunk. In the 32-minute battle, the Allied naval force suffered 1,270 officers and men killed, with another 709 wounded. Japanese losses were 35 killed and 57 wounded.

Despite this bloodying of the Americans and Australians, the Japanese were not able to drive off the enemy naval force. By shuttling men and supplies in to their garrison by night, the Japanese were able to maintain a strong grip on part of Guadalcanal. On some nights their big-gun ships took advantage of the absence of Allied air cover and bombarded the marines at Henderson Field, as the air strip had been named. By day, the carrier planes from *Wasp*, *Saratoga* and *Enterprise* returned to the air over Iron-bottom Sound, as the waters adjacent to Guadalcanal had come to be called after the losses at Savo Island.

On 24 August the Japanese tried to regain the initiative from the Americans with a reinforcement of the garrison on western Guadalcanal. A three-carrier force covered the troop ships. Admiral Yamamoto had decided that the best way to draw the defending American carrier planes into a decisive action would be to set a trap. Thus he ordered the light carrier *Ryujo* to steam in the van of the Japanese force and launch bombers against Henderson Field. At the same time, *Ryujo* was to act as the bait for the trap because Yamamoto positioned his two big carriers, *Shokaku* and *Zuikaku*, and their escorts some 60 miles behind the *Ryujo*. If all went according to plan, planes from the two big carriers would smash the American carriers while their own planes were attacking the vulnerable *Ryujo*. Once *Enterprise*, *Wasp* and *Saratoga* had been dealt with, the Japanese planners were confident they could drive the marines and their Cactus Air Force ("Cactus" was the code name for Guadalcanal) from the island.

Although Admiral Fletcher was unsure of the exact location of the Japanese carrier force, he did not expect a battle in the immediate future. Hence he detached *Wasp* and her escorts to the south for refueling. That left *Enterprise* and *Saratoga* guarding the eastward approaches to Guadalcanal at the very moment when the Japanese force was heading to attack.

About 9 A.M. on 24 August an American PBY on patrol spotted *Ryujo*. Admiral Fletcher had soon received this intelligence, and he went for the bait, launching 38 bombers and torpedo planes on an attack. Although Japanese scout planes had also located the two American carriers, Fletcher ordered his forces to close the range on *Ryujo*. At the same time, *Zuikaku* and *Shokaku* headed to the south, closing in on the Americans. As Fletcher's planes in this carrier-versus-carrier battle took Yamamoto's bait, the Japanese mounted a counterstrike against *Enterprise* and *Saratoga*. Too late, Fletcher received reports of the position of *Shokaku* and *Zuikaku*. Planes from *Saratoga* were already attacking *Ryujo* and could not be diverted for attacks on the two big carriers.

Realizing the danger of his exposed position, Fletcher ordered every available fighter into the air over his carriers. By 5 P.M. 54 Wildcats were circling over the carriers, waiting for the Japanese force of 36 Val dive-bombers and 12 Kate torpedo planes and its heavy escort of Zeros. As Wildcats and Zeros clashed at 12,000 feet, a few Kates and Vals tried to get in low over the water, but the fighter director on the "Big E" spotted them on radar and vectored out a section of his CAP (combat air patrol), which intercepted the attackers. Ensign G. W. Brooks splashed a Val and a Kate,

24 August 1942: a bomb explodes on the "Big E." The photographer was killed while taking this picture

while another ensign downed a Val. In the ensuing melee, the Wildcats shot down several more planes and forced the rest to turn tail back to their carriers.

Meanwhile, the remaining Kates and Vals continued on toward their targets. Some of them would never get to drop their bombs or torpedoes, because a few Wildcats were able to evade the Zeros and shoot them down. As the attackers approached closer and closer, the men on the carriers and their escorts waited at battle stations. At 5:12 P.M. the Vals pushed over for their dive-bombing runs. The antiaircraft batteries on the Big E and the *Saratoga* and their escorts responded with one voice.

Not all the attackers got through, but enough made it to hit *Enterprise* with three bombs. *Saratoga*, which was 10 miles away from the Big E, was not damaged by the attack. The bombs that hit *Enterprise* were deadly. The first crashed through part of the forward elevator, penetrating 42 feet into the ship before its 1,000 pounds of dynamite exploded. The ship reeled under the force of this blow. Thirty-five men died when the bomb exploded. The flight deck rippled under the concussion, and the sea entered outboard storerooms through six-foot holes in the ship's sides at the waterline.

Then a second bomb hit within 15 feet of the first. More fire, smoke, damage and death followed. This bomb killed 39 men instantly. *Enterprise* began to list. At 5:16 P.M. the third bomb crashed into the Big E on the flight deck aft of the island. Luckily, this 500-pound bomb was defective and only blew a 10-foot hole in the flight deck, though the explosion put the nearby Number Two elevator out of commission.

The damage control teams on the Big E immediately went to work trying to quench the fires, restore vital services and stop the flooding below decks. Through skill and training, they managed to contain the flooding and put out the fires sufficiently for the carrier to recover some of its planes at 5:49 P.M. But the day's troubles were not over for the crew of the Big E, because the delayed effects of these bomb hits began to take hold of the ship. When the rudder became jammed, *Enterprise* lost steering power and began to circle helplessly to starboard. As she slowed to 10 knots, a repair party set about fixing the rudder. At the same time, the air search radar began to display the telltale blips of an incoming enemy attack 50 miles away.

The temperature in the after steering room, which housed the steering engines, reached a supertorrid 170°—so exhaustingly hot that none of the seven-man engine-room gang, whose General Quarters stations were there, were strong enough to be able to make the necessary switch over to the alternate steering engine. Two machinist's mates, Chief William A. Smith and First Class Petty Officer Cecil S. Robinson, donned rescue breathing devices and headed down the access trunk to after steering. Another sailor, Fireman Third Class Ernest R. Visto, volunteered to go after the seven engineers who were unable to get themselves out of that oven. While Visto was working with the half-conscious men, the two machinist's mates sized up the problems and deftly made the switch to the alternate steering engine. Only 38 minutes after the helmsman on the bridge had lost steering, he was able to report that he had regained steering control and was ready to answer all orders to the helm. As Machinist's Mates Smith and Robinson were repairing the steering gear, the second attack wave of 30 Val dive-bombers from *Shokaku* and *Zuikaku* flew right by the Big E—50 miles away—missing the opportunity to finish her off.

Seventy-four men died on *Enterprise* as a result of the Japanese attack, but their sacrifice did not go completely unreturned. The planes from *Saratoga* that had jumped at Yamamoto's bait had not failed. *Ryujo* sank that night as a result of damage from the American attack.

Saratoga, which had emerged from this battle without serious damage, fell victim to a submarine attack on 31 August. Although she was not sunk, the torpedo damage forced her to withdraw from the area for the next three months while she was repaired. Similarly, *Enterprise* limped back to Pearl Harbor, leaving only *Wasp* and the newly arrived *Hornet* to protect the marines on Guadalcanal. *Wasp,* which had missed the Battle of the Eastern Solomons, as this last engagement is called, soon fell afoul of a Japanese submarine. While providing air cover for a convoy of transports en route to reinforce Guadalcanal, *Wasp* took three torpedo hits. Unable to control the damage and flooding, she sank on 15 September. This left *Hornet* as the only operational carrier in the area of the Solomon Islands.

In this critical situation, repairs on *Enterprise* were quickly made. En route to the Solomons, her crew and air group drilled at tasks that would soon be vitally important to them. Each day at sunrise and dusk the whole ship went to battle stations, because these are the two times when daylight is uncertain and enemy submarines could see a carrier force while remaining nearly invisible to the lookouts on the flattop and on her escorts. The carrier skipper could take no chances when the light was growing or fading.

In the South Pacific, the sea water temperature is normally around 85°; the weather is hot and humid. Even when the carrier steamed into the wind at 20 knots or more, the temperatures on the flight deck under the tropic sun could be above 90°; they might be well over 100° in the living and working spaces below decks. In the engine rooms, the heat could easily reach 120°. In the older carriers, there was no air conditioning to relieve the men from this enervating heat or the constant irritation of prickly rash and clothing damp from perspiration.

As *Enterprise* headed for Guadalcanal, the pilots and crews in her air group carried out practice shooting, bombing and torpedo runs almost daily. This training routine applied to both ground training and actual flying. When not in the air, the pilots attended classes where lectures and exercises honed their skills in tactics, weaponry and navigation. While the air group carried out its constant training, the ship's company drilled at gunnery, damage control, communications, first aid and other exercises. Frequently the gun crews would "practice fire" at the carrier's own planes, sharpening their skill at loading, tracking and firing the 5-inch guns, through dry runs in which no ammunition was actually fired. Other sailors, who normally manned the 20-mm and 1.1-inch automatic weapons during general quarters, improved their skills by firing at skeet targets. Sometimes one of the ship's aircraft would tow a sleeve on a long wire so that the carrier's gunners could actually fire at a moving target. This was especially helpful for the men who manned the 5-inch guns, which had to track a target visually.

Frequently the scout and fighter planes would make practice firing runs on a sleeve target towed overhead. Sometimes the torpedo planes would fly mock attacks with light flash bombs on a sled towed 1,000 feet astern of the carrier.

Normally each carrier squadron had models of enemy ships, and many conscientious pilots studied every detail. They would stand on chairs so that they could better recognize a particular carrier, cruiser or battleship when they saw the real ship at 12,000 feet or more. At other times, the pilots would place these ship models on a piece of painted canvas representing the ocean's surface. Various rings were drawn on this simulated ocean to mark distances of 1,000 yards. An arrow indicated wind direction; other indicators gave the courses and speeds of the model ships. Once this model fleet had been assembled, the skipper of a squadron would question his men about how they would make torpedo or bombing attacks on this force, or escape fighter interception, or return after making their attacks. Questions about the timing of an attack, various communications procedures and defensive measures were an integral part of these drills, all of which were designed to improve the pilots' skills.

One air maneuver that *Enterprise* fighter pilots practiced en route to Guadalcanal was the Thach weave, named for Lieutenant Commander John S. ("Jimmy") Thach, who had been skipper of Fighting Three (*Enterprise*'s fighters) at Midway. Thach and Lieutenant Commander Jimmy Flatley, commanding officer of Fighting Ten ("The Grim Reapers"), had found that one way the Wildcat pilots could neutralize the greater speed and maneuverability of the Zero in combat was to execute a defensive, scissoring flying pattern or weave. Since a fighter pilot could not see his own tail, each

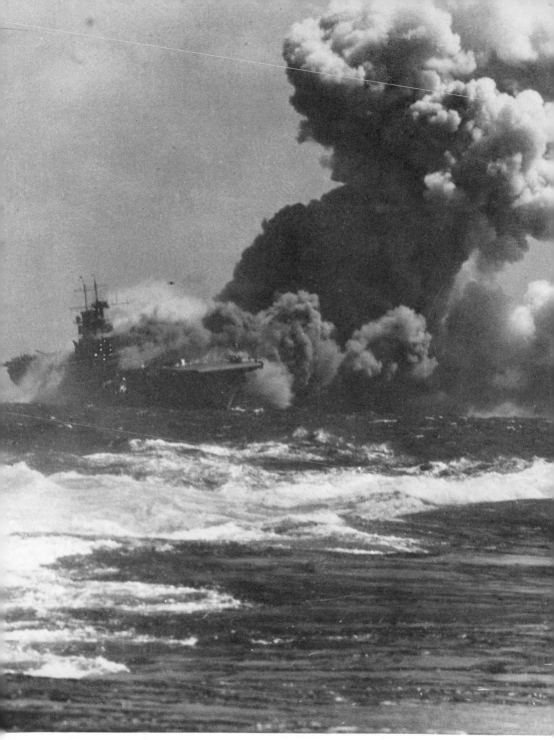

Wasp blazes after taking torpedo hits

of two pilots would protect the other's. When a Zero would begin a run on the tail of one Wildcat, the other Wildcat pilot, who was flying alongside, would alter course toward his buddy's tail, bringing the guns of the turning Wildcat onto the enemy plane. As the turning Wildcat headed toward the tail of the first, the pilot of the first would see this maneuver and would swing his plane in the direction of his squadron mate. This scissoring maneuver would put the Zero in line with the second plane's sights. Usually the Zero pilot would recognize that he was in the second Wildcat's line of fire and would quickly break off the attack to avoid being shot down.

Pilots and aircrews in both carrier navies trained hard and used drills like these to sharpen their flying skills. Japanese naval pilots went through an elaborate and grueling program in the years prior to 1942. Saburo Sakai reports that of the 70 men who began air training in his class, only 25 actually graduated. Those 70 had been culled from 1,500 applicants, but even within that elite group 45 were found to be unqualified for various reasons.

Sakai says that this hard training routine did in fact produce superior pilots. To develop the keen eyesight necessary for spotting enemy aircraft students would try to find stars visible during daylight. The routine included rigorous physical training, such as acrobatics and balancing on the head for over five minutes. Another exercise, designed to shorten reaction time and improve certainty of movement, was to catch a fly on the wing within the fists. Sakai sums up the purpose of this training when he says

The Big E at flight quarters

that "the ability to make sudden and exact movements is indispensable within the cramped confines of a fighter-plane cockpit."

As *Enterprise* steamed toward Guadalcanal, her airmen worked hard at readying themselves for the battles ahead. The goal of all these drills and exercises was probably best summed up by fighter pilot Jimmy Thach: "Fighting is a combination of instinct and brainwork. It is a combination of doing what you have learned to do automatically, and at the same time making adjustments for the various changes in the situation as they come up."

Saburo Sakai would probably have agreed with Thach's emphasis on instinct and brainwork as essential parts of a pilot's training. Sometimes, however, all the American pilots' training was still not adequate. Sakai, for one, has stated that the pilots in his air corps who met the U.S. carrier planes over Guadalcanal had never "encountered such determined opposition or faced an enemy who would not yield." But brave as these carrier pilots were, that quality was not enough; although the Americans' "tactics were wise . . . [their] gunnery was sadly deficit. Only one Zero fighter fell before these attacks."

Since air combat, especially between two fighters, demanded both instinct and brainwork, many squadron skippers like Jimmy Thach constantly drilled their men in all aspects of air operations and combat. Thach believed that for fighter pilots

> "the only way to win is by thinking faster and more accurately than your enemy: you will get him if you have equal performance and are a better pilot and marksman. I don't think it's possible to win otherwise, except by accident, and those accidents just don't happen."

Enterprise and her air group reached the seas east of Guadalcanal on 23 October and immediately joined up with *Hornet*. Rear Admiral Thomas C. Kinkaid, who had replaced Admiral Fletcher, commanded the two-carrier force, whose job was to protect Guadalcanal from the four Japanese carriers—*Shokaku, Zuikaku, Zuiho* and *Junyo*—that were operating in that area. The Japanese goal remained the recapturing of Henderson Field, but their army was making no progress against the U.S. Marines. In the meantime, Yamamoto's fleet was running low on fuel and would have to make its move shortly. It did so, but in response to an American initiative.

When Admiral Halsey, who had replaced Ghormley as Commander in Chief, South Pacific, learned early in the morning of 26 October that a PBY had located the Japanese carrier force, he flashed a three-word message to Kinkaid:

ATTACK—REPEAT—ATTACK

Search planes immediately flew off *Enterprise*'s deck and quickly located the light carrier *Zuiho*. Lieutenant Stockton Birney Strong and Ensign Charles Irvine in SBDs attacked from an up-sun position, catching the carrier's gunners and fighter cover unawares. Their bold attack worked beautifully. They laid two 500-pound bombs on the carrier's stern, ripping open the flight deck and putting her out of the battle.

While *Zuiho* was under attack by Strong and Irvine, Kinkaid's carriers were having all they could handle in a Japanese attack. Since both *Enterprise* and *Hornet* had flown off strikes against the newly located *Shokaku*, *Zuikaku* and *Junyo*, neither U.S. carrier had adequate fighter protection overhead. Sixty-five planes from the three enemy carriers swarmed over *Hornet* and *Enterprise*. The fighter director officer and his radar team had only 38 Wildcats for air defense. Hence the task force's escorts were ordered to close in, thus forming tighter rings around their two charges, so that their antiaircraft fire would be more effectively concentrated.

As *Enterprise* passed under a rain squall, the Japanese planes missed her and then turned their deadly fury on *Hornet*. The Wildcats desperately tried to break up the attack, but there were not enough of them. The ships' gunners downed some of the attackers as they came in on *Hornet*, but Lieutenant Jiichiro Imajuku from *Zuikaku* led the Kate torpedo bombers down toward *Hornet* on receiving the command "All planes go in" from the attack group commander, Lieutenant Commander Mamoru Seki of the *Shokaku*. Neither pilot survived the attack, but Seki probably was the pilot who dove his crippled plane through *Hornet*'s flight deck with two big bombs.

Hornet was in trouble. Besides the two bombs from the suicide plane, she suffered hits from four bombs, two torpedoes and another suicide plane. Twice more the Japanese launched attacks on *Enterprise* and *Hornet*. As soon as the returning Japanese planes could be refueled and rearmed, they were ordered back in the air for another attack on the Americans. One Japanese after-action report of the fighting over the American task force stated that the "battle proved so intense and enemy opposition so severe that the bomber crews were unable to assess the results of their attacks."

The results were devastating to *Hornet*. The bombs and torpedoes set her ablaze and flooded her fire rooms. Dead in the water, without power or communications, she was finished. Although she was out of the battle, *Hornet*'s planes had, in the meantime, found *Shokaku* and badly damaged her.

With *Hornet* crippled beyond repair, only *Enterprise* was left. She had not escaped the second Japanese attack unscathed. The antiaircraft light cruiser *San Juan* and the new battleship *South Dakota* valiantly tried to

Japanese attacker is about
to release its torpedo

Hornet is pounded by bombs and torpedoes

protect the Big E against those planes that got past her Wildcats, but even the 100 guns of *South Dakota* were not able to shoot down every attacker. One 550-pound bomb hit *Enterprise's* flight deck and passed through the port side of the ship, setting fires and spraying fragments in all directions. A second bomb hit aft of the forward elevator, destroying planes and killing 40 men. The last bomb that hit the ship struck her aft of the island on the starboard side, shaking her violently as it exploded.

Despite the wounds from these bombs, the "Big E" continued to function as a warship. Her engine room maintained a speed of 27 knots, and the repair parties went to work fighting the fires and aiding the wounded. While they fought this death and destruction, the *Enterprise's* skipper, Captain Osborn B. Hardison, continued to fight the Japanese. Torpedo bombers from *Shokaku* and *Zuikaku* streaked toward the carrier from both sides of the bow. The antiaircraft gunners downed four, but the others maneuvered to drop their fish—six to port, three to starboard. Captain Hardison quickly saw that the ones to starboard were the first threat and he ordered right full rudder. As the bow of *Enterprise* slowly came around to her new heading, Hardison ordered rudder amidships and the three torpedoes passed harmlessly down the carrier's portside a mere 10 yards away.

Meanwhile, the other Kates kept coming, determined to get *Enterprise* at last. They had not, however, expected to meet Lieutenant Stanley W. ("Swede") Vejtasa in one of the carrier's Wildcats. As though acting as the personal defender of the Big E, Vejtasa broke up the torpedo attack, shooting down enemy planes, forcing others to jettison their torpedoes in order to escape. When the day's action was over, Swede Vejtasa was credited with downing two Japanese dive-bombers, splashing five torpedo planes and making another probable kill. The planes which he failed to shoot down were, in the words of the skipper of Fighting Ten, Lieutenant Commander Jimmy Flatley, "so demoralized that they were ineffective." Thus *Enterprise* escaped further damage because Captain Hardison, through flawless shiphandling, evaded nine torpedoes and Swede Vejtasa took care of the rest of the Japanese attackers.

Afloat but damaged, *Enterprise* and her escorts withdrew to the south, leaving *Hornet* to be sunk by the Japanese after she had been abandoned by her crew. The Battle of Santa Cruz, as this action was called, was costly for both fleets. The Japanese carriers *Zuiho* and *Shokaku* suffered heavy damage and Yamamoto's fleet lost 100 planes. The U.S. Navy lost *Hornet* and the destroyer *Porter* and 74 planes.

The casualty and damage figures do not tell the whole story of the battle, however. The marines held once more on Guadalcanal against a Japanese army whose naval counterparts had failed to gain control of the sea. Even though the Japanese kept trying to retake Henderson Field throughout the rest of 1942, they were thrown back each time. Finally the Japanese high command gave up and gradually withdrew 12,000 troops from Guadalcanal, thereby abandoning the island to the Americans. The end of the Guadalcanal campaign—early February 1943—brought with it a pause in the pace of military operations, as both sides turned to the task of rebuilding their damaged fleets and air forces and to planning for future campaigns.

7. The Fast Carrier Task Force in Action

The Allied campaign to capture the key Japanese base at Rabaul in the Solomons took 20 long months, and in the end it was not conquered but bypassed. By March 1944 the combined forces of General MacArthur and Admiral Halsey had effectively neutralized it. With Rabaul out of the way, MacArthur was one step closer to the Philippines, which he saw as the springboard to Japan itself.

The defense of Rabaul and the Solomons had been extremely costly to the Japanese. Because Allied land- and carrier-based planes had destroyed the bulk of their air power in the Solomons-Bougainville-Rabaul area, the Japanese high command had stripped its carriers of aircraft and put them ashore to defend Rabaul. Fifty percent of its carrier-based fighters, 85 percent of its dive-bombers and 90 percent of its torpedo planes were committed to the defense of the Solomons. With these planes now flying from airfields ashore, the Japanese carriers were extremely vulnerable. Consequently they had to return to Japan to train new pilots and replace their aircraft.

While the Japanese carrier fleet suffered as a result of the Rabaul campaign, the fast carrier force of the U.S. Navy began to take shape. The campaign against Rabaul in 1943–44 gave the Americans time to build the ships and aircraft necessary to make the fast carriers a weapon of great potency. This period of building and training meant that when the U.S. Navy went on the offensive in the Central Pacific, it would have sufficient resources for a sustained drive against the enemy.

The chief naval leader and strategist of the Central Pacific offensive was Admiral Nimitz. He had orders from the Joint Chiefs of Staff in Washington to begin a second drive toward Japan through the island chains west of Hawaii. Although there were Allied leaders who believed that MacArthur's plan to strike Japan through the Solomons, New Guinea and the Philippines was strategically better, Nimitz and Admiral King had long supported a Central Pacific drive. In contrast to MacArthur's route, where the path of advance was more predictable, Nimitz and King argued that an offensive in the Central Pacific would force Japan to fragment its power because it could not be sure where the United States would strike next. In addition, they emphasized the advantages of good climate, shorter lines of communication and supply and the speed with which the war could be brought to Japanese home waters through the Central Pacific.

The principal instrument of the offensive in the Central Pacific was the U.S. Fifth Fleet, an assemblage of ships, planes and men that was so labeled in January 1944. The vanguard of the Fifth Fleet was the Fast Carrier Task Force, whose operational mission was to isolate enemy beachheads by providing preinvasion attacks and tactical air support of assault forces, and by intercepting any enemy air or surface attacks on American assault forces.

Besides the Fast Carrier Task Force, the Fifth Fleet included an amphibious force commanded by Rear Admiral Richmond Kelly Turner, which would actually carry out landings on those Japanese islands that had to be taken in the drive westward. Turner's "gator navy," as the amphibians were called, included transports, cargo vessels, landing ships, beach craft, destroyers, escort carriers for antisubmarine and air support missions, cruisers and battleships as well as Army and Marine troops who would make the assaults.

The Fifth Fleet had two other components, land-based air and the Service Force, which were essential to its operations. The planes of the land-based air forces carried out reconnaissance, photographic, patrol, defense and rescue missions. The ships of the service squadrons assigned to Fifth Fleet carried the vast quantity of supplies necessary to support the U.S. Navy's afloat forces and forward bases. Thus the Service Force consisted of supply ships, refrigerated stores ships, oilers, ammunition ships,

99

Admirals Spruance, King, Nimitz meet on a
Pacific airstrip

tenders, repairs ships and even floating drydocks that could be moved to an advanced base for quick repair of battle-damaged ships.

The emergence of the Fast Carrier Task Force as the principal weapon of the Fifth Fleet was not happenstance. It was primarily the result of the tactical principles evolving from the air and sea war with Japan. Initially the fast carriers of the U.S. Navy had been "weapons of expediency" which were used to defend Allied bases or lines of supply and to escort convoys. Until May 1942 and the Battle of the Coral Sea, these fast carriers normally operated as task forces of single carriers. Coral Sea, Midway and operations in the Solomons in late 1942 hastened the development of multicarrier task forces, in which several carriers operated together with a common screen of escorts.

The carrier-versus-carrier Battles of the Eastern Solomons and Santa Cruz helped American naval leaders clarify their operating doctrine for carriers. Thus Rear Admiral Frank Jack Fletcher argued in favor of tactical concentration of carriers after his experiences in the Battle of the Eastern Solomons (24 August 1942). Fletcher thought the "advantages to be gained from such a concentration of air power [by operating several carrier task groups together] would more than offset any disadvantages." Fletcher's

100

PBY Catalina patrol plane starts its
mission at sunset

successor, Rear Admiral Thomas C. Kinkaid, wrote following the Battle of Santa Cruz (26 October 1942) that

> "by having two carriers together one carrier can take care of all routine flying while the other maintains her full striking group spotted and ready to launch on short notice. If carriers are separated, then each must fly its own inner air patrol and combat air patrol and make its own search."

In effect, Kinkaid was arguing against a duplication of effort and in favor of a maximum coordination of air operations.

A second advantage of carrier concentration, in addition to maximum striking power, was a more effective concentration of antiaircraft fire when the Japanese attacked. At the Coral Sea, *Lexington* and *Yorktown* had separated from each other without plan. This divided the antiaircraft fire of their screening ships. Subsequent combat experience showed, however, that both carriers and escorts could defend themselves more effectively against enemy attack when they stayed together. Generally, the carriers

Pilots on standby in the ready room

absorbed the brunt of the enemy attack which left the supporting vessels free to help the flattops. Similarly, the constant availability of friendly aircraft from the carriers helped to protect the escorts.

The evolution of fast carrier doctrine and the subsequent emphasis on carrier concentration during enemy air attack received an important assist when new *Essex*-class carriers became available, beginning in May 1943. The USS *Essex* (CV-9) and other carriers of her class—such as the new *Yorktown* and the new *Lexington*—as well as the new light carriers *Belleau Wood, Cowpens, Monterey* and *Independence* joined the old-timers, *Saratoga* and *Enterprise*, in Nimitz's fleet. The light carriers (built on cruiser hulls) displaced only 10,000 tons and carried 24 fighters and nine torpedo bombers. They had a maximum speed of 32 knots. In contrast, the *Essex*-class flattops displaced 27,000 tons and carried three squadrons of fighters, scout/dive-bombers and torpedo planes (total 90–100 aircraft); they could do over 30 knots. The *Essex* and her sister ships carried over 3,100 officers and men, about twice the number on a light carrier. In addition, each ship type also carried the officers and men of her embarked air group. If an admiral was embarked on an *Essex*-class ship, there would also be the flag staff.

In the 1920s and '30s, a carrier air group (later called the carrier air wing) consisted of four squadrons—fighter, bomber, torpedo and scout. Normally a particular carrier air group (CAG) was embarked on a specific carrier. Consequently each CAG took on the name of that carrier. Thus Carrier Air Group *Enterprise*, serving aboard U.S.S. *Enterprise* (CV-6) consisted of Bombing Six, Fighting Six, Torpedo Six and Scouting Six. These numerical designations were informal only. This system worked satisfactorily as long as there were only eight aircraft carriers in the U.S. Navy. But battle losses together with the great wartime expansion of the Navy meant that a new system had to be devised. No longer could there be a simple one-to-one relationship of CAG and carrier. Hence in 1942 formal numerical designation of carrier air groups was adopted.

Each man, whether in the ship's company or the air group or on the flag staff, had an assigned station for General Quarters, which took precedence over any other job. Whether sleeping, eating, showering or working on paperwork or a pump, every man aboard a carrier ran to his General Quarters station when the alarm sounded. As Lieutenant Commander Joseph Bryan recalled it, the course from his stateroom to battle station on the flag bridge was like this:

"Run forward about seventy-five feet and up the ladder to the hangar deck, then run aft about twenty feet and up two ladders to the gallery deck; run forward

103

twenty feet, up a ladder to the flight deck, up another to the first superstructure deck, and up another to flag bridge—six (*puff!*) steep (*wheeze!*) ladders (*cough!*)."

For a member of the ship's crew, the obstacle course, whether up or down, could be even longer. Normally every ship under way went to battle stations at least at dawn and dusk. When operating in waters where contact with enemy planes or submarines was a regular occurrence, General Quarters might be manned as many as six times in a single day.

The incessant clanging of the General Quarters alarm would invariably spur a carrier's flight deck crew to even greater activity than their customary fast pace. Orders would be passed for additional planes to be launched. The pilots who would man these planes would probably be standing by in their squadron ready room on the hangar deck. Each squadron on the ship had a ready room, which was like a school classroom, having rows of seats with arm tables for writing. Standard equipment in the ready room included a chalkboard, a lectern, a teletype for message traffic and a large coffee pot. While waiting there, each pilot went over his flight plans or assignments and checked his gear—his helmet, chartboard, note pad, shoulder holster, backpack, life jacket, canteen, goggles, knife, cigarettes, lighter, handkerchief and good-luck piece. The pilots also got any last-minute instructions or weather data. When the order came to man their planes, each had to sprint up a ladder to the flight deck and climb into the cockpit of a waiting aircraft. Since a Navy pilot, unlike his Army Air Force counterpart, had no personal plane of his own, he would settle himself in the cockpit of a plane like all the others of its type. Generally no colorful drawings or slogans were found on carrier planes, because a single pilot might fly several different aircraft on successive missions. While he made his last-minute checks, aviation ordnancemen would make sure he was ready and the plane running smoothly.

Life on a carrier flight deck was a dangerous business. Whirling propellers could kill officers and flight deck crewmen with horrible suddenness. When the deck was wet and slippery or flight operations took place in predawn light or at dusk, accidents were even harder to avoid. In poor light, the taxi crews used red and green flashlights to signal which way each pilot should move his plane for takeoff, rather than relying on hand signals. Joseph Bryan captured the dangers that were always present there: "Tolerances on a live flight deck are always small, but now they are infinitesimal. An instant's inattention, a slip or even a lurch, an extravagant gesture, and a man loses a limb or his life to those murderous propellers. No actuary on earth could list all the ways that you could get killed or maimed on a live flight deck. I once saw a crewman standing just in front of an SBD's port wing, where the Pitot tube [used to measure air speed] sticks out like a lance tip. The pilot of the plane ahead suddenly gunned his engine. The crewman was blown off balance, and the Pitot tube tore his ear and gouged his cheek." Dressed in dungaree shirts and trousers with yellow oilcloth-like overshirts tied at the waist, members of the flight deck crew deftly directed the movements of each plane on deck. Other men, who wore orange overshirts, were responsible for stowing planes below, or bringing them on deck in the ship's elevators, or moving weapons or fueling hoses about the deck.

When all was ready, each pilot, in turn, released his brakes and headed his plane down the deck, accelerating to take-off speed. In daylight a pilot generally had no trouble, but in poor light or at night a takeoff required skill and coolness. When a squadron lifted off a carrier at night, few lights illumined the deck because the vessel would steam at the condition called "darken ship." Once in the air, each pilot had to strain to catch up with his squadron mates; the tail of each plane showed only a single, small white light. By day or night, the flight deck was certainly center stage on a carrier, but equally important were the activities backstage. Backstage on a carrier was the rest of the ship, principally the ship's island. Located always to starboard on U.S. Navy carriers, the island rose high above the flight deck. On an *Essex*-class flattop, the ship's twin bridges—the flag bridge surmounted by the captain's bridge—were situated 315 feet from the bow and 545 feet from the stern. The captain's bridge was the central command post from which he and the officers on watch operated the ship. One level below the captain's bridge was the flag and signal bridge, 80 feet above the flight deck. This was the battle headquarters for the admiral, if one was embarked. Adjoining the bridge was flag plot, a tiny space crammed with radar repeaters, squawk boxes, status boards and other equipment that served as the nerve center for the task force. Nearby the signalmen could communicate with ships in the immediate vicinity by flag hoist, flashing light or semaphore. When the carrier commenced launching or recovering aircraft, these "roof rats," as the signalmen were called, would two-block—hoist to the top—the Fox signal, a large red diamond on a white background, so that all the ships in company would know that she was at flight operations.

Close by flag plot were two other centers of activity, gunnery control and the air officer's control post. The air officer on each carrier directed flight operations. He coordinated takeoffs and landings and the activities of the planes on deck. Gunnery control directed the ship's antiaircraft fire. The radio shack, which was the ship's communications center, and air plot

Flight deck crew prepares to launch SBDs

were also tucked in with these posts at the level of the flag bridge. Air plot housed the Fighter Director Officer (FDO) and his assistants, who dispensed the latest information or orders to pilots and aircrews about to take off or already in the air. Just a short walk away from air plot was the photo lab, in which air intelligence officers studied photographs of the damage done on a raid just completed or analyzed photo intelligence related to a future target.

Scattered about the ship on the various bridges, in air plot and in the Combat Information Center (abbreviated to CIC and located below the flight deck on the gallery deck) were radar repeaters. These scopes, which looked like circular television tubes, displayed various blips of light indicating the disposition of both surface and air contacts. Friendly contacts were tracked at regular intervals with the information concerning them tabulated on various plexiglass status boards. Each unknown air contact, called a "bogey," and each unidentified surface contact (a "skunk") was also tracked. Once the task force determined that a bogey was an enemy plane, it became a "bandit."

The task of tracking bogeys and bandits belonged to CIC. When, for example, a phone talker in CIC had information about a fighter pursuing a bogey, he would pass it on to the bridge, flag plot and other stations by giving the bearing and range in the following manner: "Bogey 359 [degrees], 54 [miles] . . . 000, 57 . . . the CAP is closing . . . the plots have merged . . . Tallyho! . . . Splash two Bettys!" These radars, in combination with reliable communications systems, were essential to multicarrier operations.

In Admiral Spruance's Fifth Fleet, Task Force 50 formed the spearhead for the assault on Makin and Tarawa in the Gilbert Islands in November 1943. It included a total of six fast carriers, five light carriers and 700 aircraft in four task groups. Another eight escort carriers assisted the

Down on the hangar deck, ordnancemen work on bombs

amphibious force with its aircraft. Thus the total number of attackers amounted to more than 200 ships with about 900 carrier-based aircraft, which eventually flew 2,278 action sorties in various missions over the Gilberts.

Control of all this activity depended upon radar and radio communications. With radar, the carriers and their escorts could execute high-speed maneuvers at any time of the day or night, in good weather or in bad, without having to depend upon visual assessment alone. Although the Japanese had installed a crude radar system on some of their big ships by the time of Midway, it was not widely available in their fleet until much later in the war. Thus they were at a severe technological disadvantage when the Fifth Fleet went on the offensive.

Radar also helped the ships of the Fast Carrier Task Force to defend themselves. Because an enemy attack could be spotted by radar long before it came within visual range, the fighter-director officer could vector his planes out to meet the attackers 30 miles or more from the carrier, and gunnery control would know the direction of an attack and the approximate time it might be within range of the ship's guns.

In 1943 a four-channel UHF radio was installed in U.S. Navy ships. Since this radio could transmit four separate conversations from a single ship, the volume of voice communications could keep up with the growing number of ships in the Fast Carrier Task Force (though radio silence was usually maintained between ships and aircraft to prevent the Japanese from locating a carrier force). UHF had another advantage as well. Because it had only a short range, it was secure from easy enemy interception. Thus one CIC could talk directly to the CIC on another ship or one of the watch standers in flag plot could speedily send out a message to the rest of the task force or to a single ship and get a fast answer. If the admiral ordered a change in course or speed, the message over the UHF radio circuit, known as Talk-Between-Ships (TBS), might go like this: "Hello, Quebec. This is Russia. Signals execute to follow, turn shackle Mike Charlie Baker unshackle. I say again, turn shackle Mike Charlie Baker unshackle. Armada and Curio acknowledge. Over." Followed by "Hello, Russia. This is Armada. Wilco. Out" and "Hello, Russia! This is Curio! *Wil*-co! Out." Basically, this simple message from Russia, the task force commander, told Quebec, the task force, to stand by for a turn to Mike Charlie Baker, a coded heading, perhaps 080°, and requested that Armada, a particular battleship, and Curio, a destroyer, acknowledge that they got the message. They did, and they said they would comply.

Even with radar and radio, frequently the carrier's aircraft were not able to shoot down all the incoming enemy planes. For close-in defense, the *Essex*-class flattops had to depend on their own guns and those of the other ships in the task force. Radar gave valuable information about enemy contacts, but in the Pacific war it was not used with much success to control antiaircraft fire. Normally all guns would be sighted visually, a task that was possible with the speeds of propeller-driven aircraft. On the *Essex* and her sister carriers, the standard antiaircraft battery consisted of 5-inch/38 guns for long-range firepower, 40-mm Swedish Bofors cannon for intermediate ranges, and Swiss 20-mm Oerlikon cannon for short-range fire.

In early 1943 the introduction of the proximity fuze (code-named VT, for "variable time") brought about a substantial improvement in U.S. Navy antiaircraft fire. Previously gunners had had to make direct contact with their shells on a target, but the VT shell used radio waves to determine when to explode. Thus a near miss could be as good as a direct hit, and the accuracy of 5-inch/38 antiaircraft fire was tripled or quadrupled as a consequence.

Despite the availability of the VT shell, the best defense against an incoming enemy attack was still the task force's own fighter patrol. This reality of carrier warfare was reemphasized in the first genuine trial of the Fast Carrier Task Force—Operation Galvanic, the assault on Tarawa and other islands in the Gilberts on 20 November 1943. Some 2,100 miles southwest of Pearl Harbor and 1,000 miles northeast of Guadalcanal, Tarawa was a key Japanese base. Prior to the beach assaults, U.S. carrier aircraft strafed the islands and pounded enemy emplacements with bombs. To facilitate this aerial bombardment, a forward air controller flew over the beach area reporting by radio where air strikes were needed or requested by the forces on the ground. Similarly, the task force commander could get accurate and speedy reports on developments on the assault beaches through the eyes of the air observer. As enemy resistance on Tarawa began to weaken following the first bloody days of the assault, the mission of the carriers became basically defensive. They were to stand by and provide air strikes where needed ashore. Although this weapon was essential to the troops ashore, who had to root out the Japanese all over the island of Tarawa, it was contrary to the essence of the carriers—their inherent mobility. By 23 November, organized resistance on Tarawa had ended, but the Japanese had not given up—the next day a submarine torpedoed the escort carrier *Liscome Bay*, taking the lives of 644 crew members.

In the days following the loss of *Liscome Bay*, planes from Task Force 50 searched for the Japanese sub. They failed to find it; instead, Japanese night torpedo attacks on the easily located carriers increased. Usually a spotter plane would drop a parachute flare over the American ships, exposing their topside crews to temporary night blindness and enhancing the chances for a successful attack.

To counter this nocturnal harassment, one squadron of Hellcat fighters on *Enterprise* broke precedent by beginning night fighter operations. Guided by the ship's radar to the vicinity of the enemy planes and then by the radar in an accompanying TBF Avenger, the Hellcat pilots took on the attackers. On 26 November a TBF piloted by Lieutenant Commander John Phillips, skipper of Torpedo Six, and two Hellcats flown by Ensign Warren A. Skon and Lieutenant Commander Edward H. ("Butch") O'Hare, commanding officer of Fighting Six and winner of the Congressional Medal of Honor for shooting down five Japanese planes off Bougainville in February 1942, took off from *Enterprise*. Although the Fighter Direction Officer vectored the planes out to the area of the enemy, they were not able to locate these bogeys visually. O'Hare reported "no contact" via his radio. Then the FDO brought the Hellcats together with the Avenger.

In the meantime, Phillips's radioman/radar operator had picked up a bogey on his radar and was helping his skipper to close on the contact by instrument flying. When he got within 500 feet of the target, Phillips picked it up visually and added power to his engine to narrow the range. At 200 yards he opened fire with his two fixed .50-caliber machine guns. The gunners on the Betty bomber fired back from tail, top and side blisters, trying to drive off the Hellcat. Flames began to appear along the wings of the bomber as Phillips pulled up, giving his tail gunner a run on the target. As he passed out of the enemy's line of fire, Phillips realized that other

Carrier crew (USS Monterey) has something to celebrate

Edward ("Butch") O'Hare in the cockpit of his F4F

bombers, in surprise and confusion, had begun firing on each other. Phillips soon reported to the FDO, "Got that one. Any more around?"

As he began to chase another contact with the aid of the FDO's instructions, Phillips heard the voice of Butch O'Hare asking him to flash his recognition lights so that the fighter pilot could join up with the TBF. Phillips told O'Hare he had another Betty in sight and then flashed his lights. The enemy plane saw the white flash and immediately began evasive maneuvers. Phillips hung on, closing the range and firing into the fleeing bomber. With a long tail of bright red flames, the bandit hit the sea.

Since no more targets appeared to be in the area, the FDO ordered all three American planes to display their recognition lights and form up on the TBF. Skon soon took position on Phillips's left, but something went wrong as O'Hare closed in on the other two planes. Phillips's tail gunner opened fire on what he thought was another unlighted target. Skon, who saw the tracers, thought they passed between his Hellcat and O'Hare's. But very shortly after the TBF's gunner ceased firing, O'Hare's plane with its lights on began to dive toward the sea. What happened to Butch O'Hare that night has never been determined for sure, but he failed to return to *Enterprise* and no search plane found anything on the calm sea the next morning. Phillips, Skon and O'Hare had flown the first successful night interception of the war, but not without serious cost—the life of Butch O'Hare.

From the Gilberts, Task Force 50 moved on to a new target, the Marshall Islands to the north of the Gilberts. Redesignated Task Force 58 in January 1944 under the command of Rear Admiral Marc A. Mitscher, it brought death and destruction to the Japanese wherever it went. Consisting of six big carriers, six light carriers and over 700 aircraft, Task Force 58 was a portent of things to come. In three days the planes from Mitscher's carriers destroyed 150 enemy aircraft at Kwajalein and Eniwetok. The Americans completely controlled the air over the Marshalls, in Operation Flintlock, just as they had earlier over the Gilberts. Nor did the Japanese fleet sortie from its base at Truk and strike back at Task Force 58. The reason why the Japanese troops on these islands received no naval support during Operations Galvanic and Flintlock was simple, according to Captain Toshikazu Ohmac, who was a staff officer for Vice Admiral Jinsaburo Ozawa:

"At Midway, although we lost some of our carriers, a large percentage of the pilots were recovered. As there were no carriers for these pilots, the air groups were reorganized and sent to Rabaul, where these groups sustained very heavy losses. At the time of the Marshalls campaign there were no qualified air groups for our carriers, and we could not commit the fleet without carriers."

By 4 February Kwajalein was in American hands. Task Force 58 moved on to prepare to hit another target, the famed Japanese naval base at Truk (rhymes with "spook"), known as the "Gibraltar of the Pacific."

Truk consisted of a dozen volcanic islands in the midst of a lagoon enclosed by a coral reef 33 miles in diameter. As a Japanese fortress, it was expected to put up much more resistance than had anything in the Gilberts and Marshalls. In the first U.S. move, fighters from the carriers hit Truk to

Direct hit destroys Japanese torpedo
bomber off Kwajalein

gain control of the air prior to bombing and torpedo attacks. After 90 minutes of fierce air-to-air combat, the planes of Task Force 58 owned the skies over the fortress. They had downed 30 enemy planes and destroyed 40 more on the ground. Then the bombers and torpedo planes went to work, blasting all the shipping and ground installations they could find.

As part of Mitscher's plan to keep the Japanese off balance, on 17 February Avengers from *Enterprise*'s Torpedo Ten launched the war's first night bombing attack on enemy shipping. Flying in from 88 miles away, the 12 TBFs each carried four 500-pound bombs. Their radar operators guided them toward the peaceful lagoon. They climbed to 1,000 feet, then dove on the assembled shipping below, releasing their bombs at 250 feet. Although the radar had guided the TBFs to their targets, each pilot depended upon visual sighting of the dark outlines below for releasing his bombs. Methodically the raiders hit the Japanese ships, despite heavy antiaircraft fire. The dawn light revealed that two tankers and six freighters had been sunk and another five merchant ships badly damaged. Then, as the TBFs departed, their place over Truk was taken by Task Force 58's dawn fighter sweep.

The bombing raid by these Avengers on Truk showed that carrier pilots, when properly trained, could operate effectively at night. Accordingly, Torpedo Ten's commanding officer, Lieutenant Commander William I. Martin, urged in his after action report that "a night air group be created immediately to operate from a CV [fast carrier] designated primarily for night operations." Others, up the chain of command from Martin, placed their favorable endorsements on his proposal.

When Task Force 58 finally altered course to the eastward away from Truk, it left behind 250 to 275 enemy aircraft destroyed or damaged and 2 light cruisers, 4 destroyers, 2 submarine tenders and 27 merchant ships sunk or damaged beyond repair. The assaults on the Gilberts and Marshalls and the raid on Truk were the U.S. Navy's first forceful steps westward across the Central Pacific toward Japan. Ahead lay the Caroline and Mariana Islands, vital links in Japan's inner line of defense. Here, both sides knew, would be the center of the action the next time the fast carriers steamed westward.

8. "The Primary Objective is the Carriers"

The tempo of combat operations of the U.S. Fifth Fleet picked up after the successful assaults on the Gilbert and Marshall Islands. In late March 1944 three of the four task groups of Task Force 58 steamed westward beyond Truk to strike Palau in the western Carolines. Palau had become an important base in Japan's inner defense ring following the American carriers' raid on Truk. Thus it was a potential threat to General MacArthur's advance in New Guinea, some 700 miles to the southwest. Task Force 58 had the job of neutralizing Palau, so that MacArthur's flank would be secure.

As the task force headed toward the target from the southwest, Japanese scout planes spotted the 11 carriers (5 CVs and 6 CVLs), 6 battleships, 15 cruisers and 48 destroyers that Admiral Mitscher commanded. With surprise gone, the pilots in the American carriers knew that targets would be harder to find and the antiaircraft fire more intense.

Despite the Japanese efforts to get their ships out of the harbor, their planes in the air and their antiaircraft defenses manned, the strikes from TF 58 hit Palau hard just as they had done at Truk. The Japanese, in turn, countered with night torpedo attacks, but the resulting damage was minimal, thanks to the alert defenses of the task force. Those ships that were fortunate enough to get out of Palau before the carrier planes arrived discovered that they had to run a gauntlet of American submarines beyond the harbor entrance if they hoped to survive.

From Palau, TF 58 retired eastward to refuel, replenish and rearm before heading back to the west. This time its orders were to neutralize Japanese airfields around Hollandia in New Guinea, where General MacArthur had scheduled an assault for 22 April. The work of finding the enemy airfields in the jungle valleys of New Guinea was not easy, especially when some mountains reached 7,000 feet; rain was also a frequent problem for pilots dependent upon visual navigation. The radar-equipped TBF Avengers, however, were well suited to solve such problems. They could handle the mountains and the rain when human eyesight could not.

Although the Japanese antiaircraft fire was voluminous, it was not very accurate. Nevertheless it did manage to down some of the planes from TF 58. In each case, the pilots tried to make it to the sea and safety rather than bail out over territory where the Japanese were not the only enemies. New Guinea could also offer several species of poisonous snakes and insects, headhunters and a host of deadly diseases.

One damaged TBF, for example, managed to get back to *Enterprise* escorted by two Hellcats from a sister carrier. The TBF could barely stay airborne. Only one wheel would lower into landing position and it just dangled there. Shot full of holes, the plane was difficult to control because the pilot could not use his flaps, his right aileron was inoperable and his airspeed indicator had been shot away. After the third pass at the flight deck of the Big E, the Landing Signal Officer (LSO) decided the TBF was in the best position for landing that was likely under the circumstances. He also knew that the carrier's flight deck crew was ready, standing by with fire hoses, foam cans, flight deck barriers up, salvage crane ready, and the hospital corpsmen at hand; thus he slashed his right paddle down and across his body to the left, indicating that the pilot should land.

The TBF hit the flight deck hard on its one wheel and then its tail. Somehow it snagged the third arresting wire, spun slightly to the right as the wing tip dug in and came to a halt with the prop chewing splinters out of the deck. Quickly the corpsmen and flight deck crew got the plane's three injured men out of the aircraft and down to sick bay for emergency treatment. In the meantime, the flight deck plane handlers cleared the TBF out of the landing area to make room for the next plane, whether sound or damaged.

Just as had happened in the assaults on the Gilberts and Marshalls, the carriers in Task Force 58 had to stay close to the objective—in this case,

F4U-1A Corsairs over the Rabaul area

Hollandia—to be available for air strikes. This meant they were easily located by Japanese night raiders. To counter these torpedo-carrying marauders, more Americans who were specially trained in night combat took to the air over the task force. One of these pilots was Lieutenant Commander Richard E. Harmer, who flew a F4U Corsair off *Enterprise*.

Shortly after sunset on 24 March, Harmer picked up a bogey on his radarscope. When he closed on it, he saw that it was a twin-engine Betty. The Japanese plane quickly spotted Harmer and began firing with its 20-

Japanese dive-bomber—the Aichi D3A2, code-named Val

millimeters. Harmer fired back with his six .50s as the Betty dove toward
the ocean surface and jettisoned its torpedo to gain more speed. Harmer
sped after this prey, firing as he closed the range. Although the dorsal
turret gunner continued to fire at the Corsair, he was ineffective. Harmer's
fire, however, had ignited the Betty's port engine. With another burst from
his guns, the plane's wings and back caught fire. The enemy guns fired
even more wildly as the plane skidded into the sea with its five-man crew.
Soon it was out of sight.

Not every pilot in TF 58 was as skillful as Harmer nor every snooper
as ill-fated as the Betty during the Hollandia operation. In the subsequent
raid on Truk, as the carriers were withdrawing from the southwest Pacific,
a number of carrier planes were shot down by Japanese fire. Not all of the
pilots or crews from the planes were lost, however, because on one day
alone the American submarine *Tang* picked up 22 aviators from TF 58
ships.

As Japanese naval power began to diminish, Admiral Nimitz was increasingly able to use submarines like *Tang* for scouting and rescue operations. Sometimes downed pilots were picked up by floatplanes catapulted

off the big cruisers or battleships. On other occasions, destroyers were able to effect rescues by lines or boats. But submarines, because they could stay on station for long periods of time, seeing without being seen, were ideal for this kind of rescue work. Usually the aviators who were picked up were soon back aboard their carriers after a day or two as guests on the sub.

These rescue operations sometimes caused a certain amount of confusion. One notable instance involved Naval Aviation Pilot First Class Winton Dumas and his radioman/tailgunner, Aviation Radioman Second Class Earl James Crow, who in the spring of 1944 were flying a scouting mission in an SBD from the carrier *Saratoga*. Japanese antiaircraft fire severed

Admiral Mitscher aboard the new *Lexington* off Saipan

their oil line, causing them to ditch in the sea. Both men got out of the SBD before it sank and into a life raft. Shortly thereafter, an American submarine spotted them in the water and rescued them. Since Dumas and Crow, like everybody else who was flying then, wore flight suits that gave no indication of rank or rate, the submariners assumed they were officers and treated them accordingly for the next two days. Only after the submarine had transferred them to *Saratoga* by breeches buoy and the carrier's crew had welcomed back one of its enlisted pilots and his tailgunner did the submarine's officers realize that they had taken their guests' commissioned status for granted. No doubt Dumas and Crow had wanted to spare their hosts any embarrassment, and hence had wasted no effort in trying to set things straight.

Once MacArthur's forces had secured control over Hollandia, Task Force 58 was ordered to action in the Central Pacific. This time it would be the vanguard for Operation Forager, the assault on the Japanese bases on Saipan, Tinian and Guam in the Mariana Islands. The Marianas were part of Japan's inner defense line, lying west of Truk and 3,000 miles from Hawaii. The Americans wanted them because they were close enough to Japan to serve as bases for B-29 bombers. In addition, they were the next step westward toward the Philippines.

Although the Japanese high command had garrisoned the Marianas with 31,629 defenders and they were well aware of their strategic importance, the assault on the islands by Fifth Fleet with its 535 ships and more than 127,000 troops caught the Japanese by surprise. They had not expected the Americans to attack Saipan so soon after the Hollandia and Southwest Pacific operations. The assault began on 11 June 1944 with preinvasion strikes by 208 fighters and eight torpedo bombers against Tinian and Saipan. This raid left more than 100 planes wrecked on the ground; thus the bulk of the Japanese air power on the islands was destroyed even before the soldiers and marines swarmed ashore after a preassault bombardment on 15 June.

One of the pilots making a bombing raid on Saipan was Lieutenant Commander William I. Martin of *Enterprise*. Flying with Martin in his Avenger were Aviation Radioman First Class J. T. Williams and Aviation Ordnanceman Second Class W. R. Hargrove, the ball-turret gunner. Their objective was a radio station on the island. As Martin began his dive on the target, he encountered heavy antiaircraft fire. When the plane reached 3,500 feet, Martin let go his 500-pound bomb, but as he did so the plane jerked and shook violently. Beginning to tumble end over end, the Avenger fell out of control. Martin tried to tell his crewmen over the microphone to bail out, but he could not find the mike. When he realized that he could not regain control and that the plane had caught fire, he

120

bailed out, landing in a lagoon along the shore in about five feet of water. His plane crashed nearby, killing both Williams and Hargrove.

As Martin pulled in his parachute, he realized that he was under fire from Japanese riflemen on shore some 200 yards away. He ducked under the surface and swam toward the reef about half a mile offshore. The Japanese pursued him in two small boats. The firing resumed each time he came up for a breath. Martin knew he had to escape not only to stay alive but also to protect the lives of other pilots. As a senior squadron commander, he was aware of information about the upcoming assault that the Japanese would wish to know—and would seek to find out.

When one of the boats had closed within 200 yards of Martin, two TBFs flew past, looking for him. They drove off one of the boats and attracted shrapnel from antiaircraft fire, most of which fell into the water near Martin. As the carriers' second strike hit targets in Saipan, the second Japanese boat was forced to give up its search for the American pilot to avoid being destroyed itself.

During this second strike, Commander Martin carefully studied the beach area in front of him. Fixing his position on easily recognized landmarks, he made mental notes about the depth of water, the current, the gradient of the beach and the location of the antiaircraft batteries. Then he hastily scrambled over the coral reef, dived into the sea beyond, and inflated his Mae West. Once clear of the reef, he inflated his rubber raft and climbed aboard.

Shortly thereafter two more friendly planes, a TBF and an F6F, came in low from the west. Martin flashed his mirror at them and spread some dye marker on the sea. He caught not only their attention but that of the defenders on shore. Quickly he slipped back into the sea to avoid the enemy fire. Soon his raft had drifted out of the range of the enemy guns. In the meantime the pilots had promptly reported that they had observed Martin making a speed of three knots on a course of 290°, not zigzagging. Not long thereafter a float seaplane (SOC) from the cruiser *Indianapolis* landed on the sea and picked up a tired Bill Martin. Safe aboard the *Indianapolis*, he delivered his hard-won intelligence information about one of Saipan's beaches to Admiral Spruance himself.

While the soldiers and marines of the Fifth Fleet were struggling to push the Japanese back toward the center of Saipan, Admiral Spruance received other news of the enemy's activities. Two American submarines, *Flying Fish* and *Seahorse*, had spotted elements of the Japanese Mobile Fleet heading toward Saipan from different directions. And on 17 June the submarine *Cavalla* reported that it had observed a large force of Japanese warships advancing on the Marianas.

Although Spruance was aware that the Japanese fleet was on the move, his intelligence information from the submarines was not definite enough for him to be sure exactly how many separate forces he might be facing. Thus he kept Admiral Mitscher and his fast carriers tethered close to Saipan to ensure that the beachhead ashore was well protected. Mitscher knew that the Japanese force, especially its carriers, held an initial advantage. The lighter Japanese planes had a longer range than the armored American planes; thus they could conceivably attack first. In addition, the Japanese were already heading into the wind on their easterly course. This meant that they could launch planes while continuing to close on the Americans. Task Force 58, in contrast, would have to steam eastward, away from the enemy, whenever it wanted to launch or recover its planes. As dawn came to the Central Pacific on 19 June, Task Force 58 was still within 100 miles of both Saipan and Guam, and it had no precise information about the position of the Japanese.

When the Americans had attacked Saipan, Admiral Toyoda, the Commander in Chief of the Japanese Combined Fleet, had ordered Vice Admiral Jinsaburo Ozawa's force to rendezvous with a second carrier force in the Philippine Sea. Toyoda hoped that this would lead to the decisive battle that would turn the tide of the war. When the two Japanese forces joined up west of Saipan on 16 June, they totaled 9 carriers, 5 battleships, 13 cruisers, 28 destroyers and 430 carrier aircraft.

Ozawa knew that the Americans had more ships and aircraft and more experienced pilots, but he counted on his favorable wind position and on land-based aircraft already in the Marianas to help him even the match. He also planned to have his planes shuttle between the carriers and bases on Guam, thereby hitting the Americans from two directions. Had Ozawa known that the Americans had destroyed all but about 30 planes in the Marianas and that they had cut off his route for aerial reinforcement from Japan and Iwo Jima—and had bombed the airfields on Guam as well—he might have been less optimistic that the Japanese could win a decisive victory.

At 10 A.M. on 19 June the radar on the ships of Task Force 58 displayed the telltale blips of bogeys 150 miles to the west. These represented the first of four raids the Mobile Fleet would launch that day. It consisted of 45 bombers, 8 torpedo planes and 16 Zeros. Mitscher closed on the Japanese for another 20 minutes and then reversed course so that he could launch 450 fighters in retaliation. After the fighters had taken off, he ordered the carrier-based bombers and torpedo bombers to hit Guam, making sure that its airfields would be unusable for the enemy carrier aircraft.

Following the orders of their fighter directors, the Hellcats of TF 58 achieved an altitude advantage in the initial phases of the air battle. Thus when the two forces clashed, the Hellcats were able to dive on the inexperienced Japanese pilots, and they shot down at least 25 of the enemy. A few attackers managed to reach the ships of TF 58, but they were blasted by antiaircraft fire. Only 27 Japanese planes got back to their carriers, while all but one of the American planes returned.

Even before the aircraft of Task Force 58 landed to rearm and refuel, those on the carriers and their escorts knew that this was their day. Already the radios on the ships had crackled with reports such as "Tallyho! Tallyho! Many bandits" . . . "Splash one Zero" . . . "Splash two Kates." The course of battle had also been displayed visually on the radarscopes in air plot, CIC and elsewhere. As the FDOs vectored the Hellcats onto the enemy planes, numerous unidentified blips suddenly disappeared from the screens.

Admiral Ozawa's second raid on the American carriers numbered 128 planes. Hellcats from Task Force 58 met them en route and quickly reduced the enemy strike to about half its initial size. Only 31 Japanese planes in this raid returned to their carriers. The final two raids were even less successful. The 47 planes in the third raid caused no damage and took seven losses. The fourth raid was an utter disaster: out of 82 aircraft, only 11 managed to return.

This slaughter was the now-famous "Great Marianas Turkey Shoot," as one quick-witted pilot named it. On this day, Lieutenant (jg) Alexander Vraciu, a Hellcat fighter pilot on *Lexington*, epitomized the superior skill and determination of the pilots of TF 58. Vraciu had learned how to handle his plane in combat from Butch O'Hare, flying as O'Hare's wingman until O'Hare had died in night action over the Solomons. After he took off on the morning of 19 June, Vraciu had trouble with his engine and lagged behind his squadron leader; thus the FDO ordered him to orbit near the carriers. Suddenly he heard the FDO's voice on the radio: "Vector 265!" That meant action. As he picked up three enemy planes ahead, Vraciu yelled "Tallyho!" into his mike and took off after them.

In the ensuing air melee between Hellcats, Zeros, Judys and Jills, Vraciu took on one enemy plane at a time, cutting it out from the others, closing it and firing when within range. With deadly accuracy he splashed six Japanese dive-bombers, the last of which he shot down while it was diving on a destroyer. Vraciu's six kills was high for his squadron, Fighting Sixteen, which shot down 44 Japanese planes altogether (Fighting Fifteen on the *Essex*, however, totaled 60 kills for the day's action). Once Vraciu was back aboard *Lexington*, Admiral Mitscher personally congratulated him and asked the photographers to take a picture of the two of them. As soon as he had made the request, Mitscher immediately added a qualification: "Not for publication. To keep for myself."

One of Mitscher's carrier task groups had orders to raid the Japanese

123

Commander David McCampbell shot down
seven Japanese planes in the "Great Turkey
Shoot." He became the Navy's all-time ace—34 kills

garrison on Iwo Jima, west of the Marianas, to make sure that no Japanese
reinforcements could be flown in from that airfield. One of the fighter
pilots on Iwo Jima was Naval Aviation Pilot First Class Saburo Sakai, who
had lost the vision in one eye in the battle for Guadalcanal. Even though
he had only one good eye, Sakai was an experienced pilot, and in one dogfight he realized that the "enemy pilots were as green as [his] own inexpe-

rienced fliers." This, he explained, was one reason he was able not only to fly several combat missions and survive, but also to down at least one Hellcat, bringing his total confirmed kills for the war to over 60 enemy planes.

Sakai's account of one of those kills over Iwo Jima was typical of his vivid descriptions of what took place:

> I snapped into a tight loop and rolled out on the tail of a Hellcat, squeezing out a burst as soon as the plane came into the range finder. He rolled away and my bullets met only empty air. I went into a left vertical spiral, and kept closing the distance, trying for a clear shot at the plane's belly. The Grumman tried to match the turn with me; for just that moment I needed, his underside filled the range finder and I squeezed out a second burst. The cannon shells exploded along the fuselage. The next second thick clouds of black smoke poured back from the airplane and it went into a wild, uncontrolled dive for the sea.

Even though Sakai got this Hellcat and another squadron mate downed four more, the Americans shot down nearly 40 of the fighters on Iwo in that raid.

With his flanks protected by raids such as the one on Iwo Jima, Mitscher was free to concentrate on the pursuit of the Japanese carriers. He knew that they had lost about 330 planes on 19 June in the "Turkey Shoot." In addition, the submarine USS *Albacore* had torpedoed and sunk Ozawa's flagship, the new fast carrier *Taiho*. Another submarine, *Cavalla*, had subsequently sunk the Pearl Harbor veteran, *Shokaku*, with a spread of three torpedoes. The loss of *Shokaku* forced Ozawa to transfer his flag to *Zuikaku*. Mitscher now judged that the time was right to pursue the retiring Japanese and finish them off.

Unfortunately, he ordered his task force to steam in a southwesterly direction during the night of 19–20 June. He believed that he was closing Ozawa's force when, in fact, he was gaining very little on the slower enemy ships. Hence most of the daylight hours on 20 June were spent searching for the Japanese. At last, about 4 P.M., a search plane from TF 58 located the Mobile Fleet, 220 miles west northwest of the American carriers.

Even though the Japanese were well beyond the optimum attack range for American carrier planes, Mitscher's order, "Launch 'em," committed a deckload of 85 fighters, 77 dive-bombers and 54 torpedo bombers to a night attack on the fleeing Japanese.

Once the first strike from Task Force 58 was in the air, Mitscher received a corrected position report on the Mobile Fleet. It was actually 60 miles farther away than had been originally reported. Some of the planes would be flying about 300 miles just to make the attack. Realizing that the flight homeward and the night landing would be extremely hazardous, Mitscher canceled plans for a second strike.

The planes from TF 58 overtook the Japanese shortly before sunset. Initially, they came upon two oilers, which a few planes attacked and sank, but the strike force was after bigger game than oilers. In the words of the air intelligence officers on the carriers, "Your primary objective is the carriers." Thus the other planes flew on until they saw the main body of the Japanese fleet.

As the Americans headed for advantageous attack positions, 75 Japanese planes met them in the air over the fleet. Simultaneously the Japanese ships opened up with all the antiaircraft fire they could muster. The darkening sky was filled with brilliant colors: green, yellow, blue, white, pink and purple, all from the thermite and phosphorous shells of the Japanese antiaircraft fire.

One member of Bombing Sixteen from *Lexington*, Lieutenant Cook Cleland, flew right through this murderous defensive fire as he made his run on a Japanese carrier. As Joseph Bryan tells it,

> "by now the anti-aircraft had the range and deflection cold. A 20-millimeter shell hit [the] right tank. A 40-millimeter hit [the] starboard wing, ripping a two-foot hole. Another 40 tore out the floor of the after cockpit. [Aviation Radioman Second Class William J.] Hisler screamed, 'Jesus! I've got the Purple Heart and no left leg!' He wasn't hurt. The hit had made his leg numb. Cleland kicked the plane back on line and dropped his bomb ten feet forward of the [carrier's] stern."

In attacks like Cleland's, the American carrier planes heavily damaged the flight decks of the carriers *Zuikaku* and *Chiyoda* and also crippled a battleship and a cruiser. Task Force 58 Avengers put one, possibly two, torpedoes into the carrier *Hiyo*, setting it afire and touching off a series of internal explosions. *Hiyo* was the only combatant actually sunk in this night attack.

Once the SBDs and Avengers had expended their bombs and torpedoes, they faced a swarm of Japanese Zeros ready to intercept them on their way home to Task Force 58. Using short, sharp changes in course and altitude—a maneuver called jinking—each pilot attempted to throw off or confuse the fire from the Zeros. Sometimes this effort worked, especially with inexperienced enemy pilots. Japanese planes and antiaircraft fire together shot down 20 of the attackers. A few of the pilots and crew members in those 20 American planes were able to jump from their planes and parachute into the sea; others, like Lieutenant (jg) James A. Shields and Aviator Radioman Second Class Leo O. LeMay, were not so lucky. They were downed by a Zero which hit Shields as he was trying to retire after his bombing run. Radioman/tailgunner LeMay kept firing at the enemy plane until his own plane hit the water.

Once clear of the Zeros, Mitscher's aviators still had to find their carriers. Low on gasoline and uncertain about the exact location of Task Force 58, they could not afford to search far for a deck to land on. Pilots with crippled or badly damaged planes were among the first to ditch on the way home. Bucking a 14-knot head wind, even the sound aircraft burned fuel disturbingly fast. In the two to three hours that it took these planes to return, the American fliers had plenty of time to think about what they should do. Voices on the radio explained individual circumstances succinctly:

"I've got ten minutes of gas left, Joe. Think I'll put her down in the water while I've still got power. So long, Joe!"

"This is Forty-six Inkwell. Where am I, please? Somebody tell me where I am!"

"Where's home, somebody? I'm lost!"

F6F Hellcat was the first U.S. plane built out of
World War II combat experience

Five pilots took a vote on what to do—keep going or ditch while they still had enough fuel to control their planes. They voted four to one to ditch. "That's that!" said the chairman. "OK. Here we go!"

Fully aware of the problems his pilots were facing on the flight home, Admiral Mitscher had his task force close the range as fast as possible. He also took a bold step to try to save lives. To Captain Arleigh Burke, his chief of staff, he gave the order, "Turn on the lights." Despite the possibility that enemy submarines or night raiders were lurking nearby, Mitscher was willing to risk those dangers to help his fliers return safely.

Immediately the task force blossomed with lights. Running lights, truck lights, glow lights to outline the flight decks as well as star shells and searchlights illuminated the area around the ships. By now the planes were approaching. Knowing that many of the pilots might not have enough gas to find their own carriers, Mitscher had air plot pass the word for them to land on any deck they could find. Methodically the Landing Signal Officers on each carrier tried to bring the struggling planes in by using red flashlights to tell each pilot what he needed to do on his approach run. In their anxiety to get down before their fuel ran out, the carrier pilots hurried their approaches, elbowing and jockeying with each other for position to land.

The LSO on *Lexington* had just landed his sixth plane when the next one, an SB2C Helldiver, did not respond to his wave-off signal. It was coming too fast and had no lights. Frantically the LSO tried to get the pilot to swerve, slow or overshoot the carrier. Otherwise he knew what would happen. Nothing worked. As the plane struck the deck, the crash siren went off. The uncontrolled aircraft crashed into four planes that had just landed and been parked on the forward part of the deck. The SB2C's bomb broke free of its brackets and rolled across the deck, while oil and gasoline gushed from the damaged planes. Two men died and six others were injured on *Lexington* as a result of this pilot's desperate attempt to land. *Bunker Hill* had a similar problem. Two aircraft disregarded the LSO's signals and crash-landed. They killed two more men and injured four others.

Some planes never got a chance to land. One ran out of gas on its approach run and gently settled into the sea astern of a carrier. The pilot and tailgunner were eventually picked up by a destroyer which the pilot alterted to their position by firing his .38-caliber pistol into the air several times. Once aboard, the pilot and tailgunner found they had company, two other pilots that the destroyer had already fished out of the Philippine Sea.

When the last plane had landed, Mitscher got the reports on the damage done to the enemy and to his own forces. *Zuikaku* damaged and *Hiyo* and two oilers sunk—the Japanese had only about 35 operable carrier

Gregory ("Pappy") Boyington, all-time Marine ace—28 kills

planes left. Task Force 58 had losses, too. Eighty American planes had either ditched or crashed on landing. That night and the next day the task force managed to rescue 160 of the 209 aviators who had taken off after the Mobile Fleet on the afternoon of 20 June.

Although Mitscher and Task Force 58 tried to catch the Japanese the next day, they were too far behind to overtake the remnants of Ozawa's Mobile Fleet. The surviving carriers would return to fight again, but they would never regain the air strength they had lost at the Marianas nor would the pilots of their replacement planes be experienced.

In the Battle of the Philippine Sea Mitscher's aggressive handling of the Fast Carrier Task Force had guarded the beachhead for the amphibious assault on Saipan and also dealt with a dangerous Japanese counterattack. And he had shown the men on the carriers of TF 58 that he cared about their welfare and that, as long as he was in command, no pilot or aircrew member was considered to be expendable.

With the fall of Saipan, Tinian and Guam, the Japanese Emperor and the political leaders decided that the Prime Minister and Army Chief of Staff, General Hideki Tojo, was expendable. The loss of the Marianas was too much, and the Tojo government fell. The Emperor indicated his desire for early peace negotiations. But before any peace could come to the combatants in the Pacific, both sides would expend many more lives in battle.

129

9. Combat-The Stars and Stripes at Leyte Gulf

For many of Japan's naval leaders, the Philippines were one area that had to be held at any cost. Once they had fallen to the enemy, the road to Tokyo would be wide open. Vice Admiral Takeo Kurita, commander of one of the Japanese naval forces that would take part in the action at Leyte Gulf, told his men prior to the opening of combat, "We are about to fight a battle which will decide the fate of the Empire."

The struggle for Leyte Gulf was not a single battle, like Midway, which took place on several successive days in a relatively small geographical area. Instead, it was a series of major naval battles fought over a wide expanse of ocean and taking nearly a week's time from preliminaries to conclusion. Some, like Admiral Frederick C. Sherman, have argued that it should be called the Second Battle of the Philippine Sea (the First Battle of the Philippine Sea having been the struggle for the Marianas), but Admiral Nimitz labeled the series of engagements off the eastern coast of the Philippines as the Battle for Leyte Gulf. Regardless of the name used, the series of battles involved surface gunnery duels, carriers-versus-carriers combat and full-blown air warfare.

131

Gun crews strain to identify a plane overhead

In September 1944 Admiral William F. Halsey took command of the U.S. Third Fleet, succeeding Admiral Spruance, who moved ashore to an assignment in Hawaii. Spruance's Fifth Fleet actually became Third Fleet with the change of command, and Task Force 58, which was still commanded by Vice Admiral Marc A. Mitscher, became Task Force 38. Mitscher served both Spruance and Halsey until he was later relieved by Vice Admiral John S. McCain. Thus Nimitz had two teams of top leaders in his Pacific Fleet—Spruance and Mitscher, Halsey and McCain—who alternated at sea.

The ships that made up TF 58/38 stayed relatively the same, regardless of who was in command. Only their operational designation changed. Although the composition of the Fast Carrier Task Force was relatively stable in this sense, other changes had occurred by the summer and fall of 1944.

By this time, the air groups aboard the carriers in Task Force 38 were weighted more heavily toward fighters than dive-bombers. In part, this was because the enemy had fewer surface vessels to serve as targets. And, increasingly, the carrier aircraft were flying missions over beachheads to support landing forces and attack enemy bases ashore. Thus a typical air group in mid-1944 consisted of 50 fighters, 4 night fighters, 24 scout/dive-bombers and 18 torpedo planes. The light carriers usually carried 24 fighters and 9 scout/dive bombers.

As in the Marianas, the Fast Carrier Task Force consisted of three or four task groups, each of which was composed of four carriers (three fast carriers and a light carrier). For antisubmarine patrol, antiaircraft defense and other escort duties, each task group would usually have two battleships, four cruisers and 16 destroyers. The number of ships in a given task group might vary from this norm, but not greatly, for the remainder of the war.

By mid-1944 some new weapons were a part of the Fast Carrier Task Force arsenal. Some of the fighters were equipped with 20-mm cannon as well as machine guns. Two aerial rockets, the 5-inch "Tiny Tim" and the 11.75-inch HVAR (high velocity aircraft rocket), which was nicknamed the "Holy Moses," were introduced to carrier aircraft. These rockets proved to be particularly useful against ground installations and troop concentrations. Napalm bombs were also first tried in 1944 as a means for ridding a target area of jungle overgrowth.

As the Americans were developing this might in ships, aircraft and weapons, the Japanese were facing increasing shortages of all sorts. U.S. submarines cut the supply line between the Philippines and the Home Islands in the fall of 1944, so that only a trickle of oil, raw materials and food reached Japan. Although the Japanese Navy still had the carriers *Hosho, Junyo, Zuikaku, Amagi, Unryu, Chitose, Chiyoda, Ryuho,* and *Zuiho,* with a total capacity of 400 aircraft, they lacked the planes and trained pilots to make these carriers fully effective. Similarly, they were short of destroyers to screen the carriers and of tankers to supply the oil needed to operate their fleet and its aircraft.

The struggle for the Philippines began in earnest in the fall of 1944 with a series of carrier raids by Task Force 38 on Japanese bases in Okinawa, Taiwan and the Philippines. In these preliminary skirmishes, Halsey's

Admirals McCain (l.) and Halsey at sea

carrier-based aircraft once again faced Japanese land-based aircraft, which placed a premium on the mobility of the carrier forces.

On 12 October 1944 Lieutenant Cecil E. Harris, flight officer of Fighting Eighteen on the fast carrier *Intrepid*, took off with his squadron mates for a strafing run on a Japanese airfield on northeast Taiwan. While en route, Harris and the members of his division chanced upon five enemy Kate bombers. Before the startled Japanese knew the Hellcat fighters were in the air, they were under attack. Harris shot down two of the bombers and the others in his division downed two more.

Then the American Hellcats realized that they were being attacked by Japanese Zeros. One Zero latched on to the tail of Lieutenant (jg) Egidio DiBatista, who had just shot down another Japanese fighter. Harris, in turn, closed on the Zero at full throttle, hoping he could get the enemy plane before it could shoot down DiBatista. As 20-mm shells hit the first Hellcat, Harris poured .50-caliber shells into the Zero. Slowly, the Zero curved away from Harris's line of fire and crashed into the trees below.

Meanwhile DiBatista reported that his Hellcat was shot up. Harris encouraged his fellow pilot to make for *Intrepid* and safety. One member of Fighting Eighteen had already been forced to bail out over enemy territory. Harris also promised that he would keep DiBatista covered while he ran for the sea. But with more than 20 Zeros in the air, Harris had his hands full. Using his own plane as bait, he decoyed a Zero into making an attack from above and behind. Then, at just the right instant, Harris gave his Hellcat left stick and rudder, throwing her into a sharp, vertical left turn. The Zero did not follow Harris, but instead went after DiBatista. With a sharp bank back to the right, Harris dove on the Zero. His wingman joined him in this maneuver, forcing the Japanese pilot to break off his attack on the crippled Hellcat. Within minutes Harris closed the gap on the Zero and downed him with another burst from his guns. By this time DiBatista was well clear of the coast and headed for *Intrepid*. Apparently the other Zero pilots realized that they were outmatched by the Hellcats and chose not to contest the air further. The Americans now headed for home, too.

In the interdiction strikes flown by Lieutenant Harris and other fighter pilots from Task Force 38, heavy damage was inflicted on Japanese ground facilities on Taiwan. Although the Americans encountered stiff antiaircraft and fighter opposition, the Japanese lost over 100 planes on 12 October. But the cost was high—48 carrier-based planes were downed. Admiral Halsey later called this period of operations over Taiwan a "knock-down, drag-out fight between carrier-based and shore-based aircraft," which was an essential preliminary to the landings at Leyte. Halsey knew that the assault

Often-hit carrier *Intrepid* earned the nick-name the "Evil I"

on the Philippines could be seriously jeopardized if the Japanese could use the airfields on Taiwan as a staging base for enemy planes bound for Leyte.

Two days after Lieutenant Harris downed four Japanese planes over Taiwan, Lieutenant Charles R. Stimpson of *Hornet*'s Fighting Eleven shot down at least five Japanese planes, and probably two more, while flying Combat Air Patrol (CAP) for *Hornet*. Following instructions from the *Hornet* fighter director, Stimpson and six other Hellcats in the CAP intercepted an incoming Japanese raid 40 miles or more from the carrier.

Catching the enemy fighters and dive-bombers by surprise, the Hellcats attacked a numerically superior Japanese force. The result was a fierce air melee between the Hellcats and Japanese Zeros, Hamps (improved Zeros with self-sealing fuel tanks), and Tonys (a new fighter that was faster than the Zero and had an in-line engine).

Although the CAP leader had radioed for help from *Hornet*, no additional Hellcats were available. Thus Stimpson and his six fellows were left to cope with about 30 Japanese planes. Their skillful flying managed to break up the enemy attack and protect *Hornet*, but as Stimpson learned

135

when he got back to the carrier, the Hellcat losses had been worse than he feared. Besides himself, only two fighters returned undamaged. One pilot made it back with serious wounds and a badly shot up plane. Three pilots failed to return and were not found by subsequent patrols.

Operating 50 to 90 miles east of Taiwan during the three days of interdiction raids on the Japanese bases there, Task Force 38 was particularly vulnerable. Just as the fighter squadrons on her carriers suffered losses in those raids, the task force itself also was damaged. Japanese attackers scored one hit on the carrier *Franklin* and one on the cruiser *Canberra*, and crippled the cruiser *Houston*, which had to be towed clear of the area. In all three cases, good work by damage control parties saved the ships.

Japanese losses in the three-day air battle were heavy. Task Force 38 destroyed over 500 enemy aircraft, sank over 20 merchant craft and destroyed many airfield installations and fuel and ammunition dumps. Despite the fact that many of the Japanese pilots had learned their air tactics only from motion picture films of attacks on model U.S. warships, their superior numbers meant that the Americans lost 79 planes, including 64 pilots and crewmen.

Originally, the Allies had planned to invade Leyte in December 1944, but carrier raids on the Philippines by Admiral Halsey's forces in September convinced the U.S. Joint Chiefs of Staff that the timetable could be accelerated. MacArthur agreed to this change provided forward bases on Morotai, Peleliu and Ulithi were secured in advance. Amphibious landings on these islands in September involved some very bloody fighting, especially on Peleliu, but eventually the U.S. Navy–Marine Corps team gained control of the islands. Ulithi subsequently became an enormous fleet base that provided logistic support for naval operations to the west.

Her spacious and well-protected lagoon held repair ships and tenders that provided all sorts of maintenance and repair facilities for Task Force 38. On the nearby island of Mog Mog, weary sailors and pilots could relax in the sun, swim and drink beer during their few hours of free time. This kind of R&R came infrequently, given the tempo of operations, but it was at least better than none at all. By the spring of 1945 the harbor of Ulithi had become so filled with all types of ships, even big carriers, that one carrierman, Lieutenant Commander Joseph Bryan, could tell how he was on a launch returning to the carrier *Lexington* one night when he met a Navy captain preparing to report to an *Essex*-class carrier as its prospective commanding officer. Unfortunately, there were so many *Essex*-class carriers at Ulithi that no one could tell for sure which one was the captain's new command, because they all looked so similar. Today the lagoon at Ulithi is not nearly so busy as in 1944–45, but traces of those days are still there. The water is so polluted, from various metal poisonings, that the natives cannot eat some kinds of local fish.

Initially, General MacArthur and Admiral Nimitz had disagreed over whether the next assault should be on the Philippines or on Taiwan. President Roosevelt accepted MacArthur's argument for the Philippines, and the assault date was set for 20 October. The landing in the Philippines had two factors in its favor: beaches at Leyte were better for amphibious operations, and no one had vowed to return to Taiwan.

For his pledged return to the Philippines, MacArthur had the ground troops of Lieutenant General Walter Krueger's Sixth Army and Vice Admiral Thomas C. Kinkaid's Seventh Fleet for transport and gunfire support in the landings. Admiral Nimitz's contribution to the assault was Admiral Halsey's Third Fleet. The invasion involved 738 ships, of which 157 were combatants (including 17 fast carriers) and 420 amphibious ships. Preliminary operations in the Leyte area on the east coast of the Philippines began on 17 October with Assault Day (A-Day) occurring three days later.

Compared with many of the amphibious assaults of World War II, the landings at Leyte were unopposed. Enemy resistance was light and by midnight on 20 October, 132,400 men and nearly 200,000 tons of supplies were ashore. MacArthur had indeed returned.

When Admiral Soemu Toyoda, Commander in Chief of the Japanese Combined Fleet, learned that the Americans had landed at Leyte, he immediately set in motion *Sho-Go I* (Victory Operation I), the defense of the Philippines. Under this plan, three separate forces were to converge on the assault area and defeat the enemy. Vice Admiral Takeo Kurita sortied from Lingga Roads, near Singapore, with a force of battleships, cruisers and destroyers and headed for the San Bernardino Strait, north of Leyte. Vice Admiral Kiyohide Shima sailed for Surigao Strait, south of Leyte, with a force of cruisers and destroyers. The third Japanese force, a group of carriers and escorts, commanded by Vice Admiral Jinsaburo Ozawa, sortied from the Japanese Inland Sea.

Even as these forces approached Leyte, the Allies were beginning to get some idea of the Japanese battle plan. En route to the Philippines, Kurita's force refueled at Brunei, Borneo. Then it was divided. Two old battleships, a heavy cruiser and four destroyers under the command of Vice Admiral Shoji Nishimura headed for the southern passage to Leyte, Surigao Strait. Kurita led the remaining ships, including the super-battleships *Yamato* and *Musashi*, for the northern passage to Leyte. Thus the Japanese hoped to catch MacArthur and his transports in a pincers from north and south. For the sake of clarity, Allied intelligence officers labeled the three Japanese forces as follows: the ships of Shima and Nishimura as

137

the Southern Forces; Kurita's ships as the Center Force; and Ozawa's carriers, once located, as the Northern Force.

Allied intelligence first discovered Kurita's Center Force on 23 October when the submarines *Darter* and *Dace* attacked it southwest of the Philippines. The two submarines torpedoed and sank the heavy cruiser *Atago*, crippled the heavy cruiser *Takao* and blew the heavy cruiser *Maya* apart when their torpedoes exploded ammunition magazines. The following day, air patrols from Halsey's carriers spotted Nishimura's ships, the van of the Southern Forces. Although the carrier planes attacked, they did not inflict serious damage on the Japanese warships.

Halsey, as commander of the Third Fleet, had Mitscher as his commander of Task Force 38, but he effectively assumed tactical command of both the fleet and the task force. Thus Mitscher was severely limited in what he might do with the carriers. The four task groups that made up Task Force 38 were spread out east of the Philippines so that they could cover the beachhead. Each task group averaged about 23 ships. Since the Japanese had not chosen to offer strong opposition to the landings, Halsey had ordered one task group to retire eastward for refueling. The others flew patrol, antisubmarine and air support missions as they steamed off Leyte.

The first significant air action by these carriers involved attacks on Kurita's Center Force as it tried to cross the Sibuyan Sea prior to entering San Bernardino Strait. Halsey, concentrating his planes, ordered five strikes at the Center Force. These attacks were devastating, especially since Kurita's repeated pleas by radio for land-based air support went unanswered, largely because U.S. carrier planes had already destroyed many of the aircraft in the Philippines and those remaining were ordered to attack the carriers. Apparently the Japanese judged their pilots might have a better chance against the American ships than against the enemy pilots. Their attacks, however, were not very successful. When Halsey got word of the location of Kurita's force, he personally gave the order that put the first planes in the air: "Strike! Repeat: Strike! Good luck!" Fighters, dive-bombers and torpedo bombers from *Intrepid* and *Cabot* soon found the Center Force.

The American strikes on Kurita's ships hit four of his battleships, put the heavy cruiser *Myoko* out of action and damaged two destroyers. The focus of the airborne attack was, of course, the superbattleships. Each of these giants had 120 25-mm antiaircraft guns, and the cruisers had 90. Yet they were unable to drive off the Americans during their repeated attacks. By early afternoon *Musashi* alone had taken one bomb hit and four torpedoes. Yet she still headed eastward as though undamaged.

As the dive-bombers and fighters from Task Force 38 grew more aggressive, the Japanese decided to use even their 18.1-inch guns for antiaircraft fire. Loading them with a special spray shell called *sanshiki-dau*, they fired them at 65 incoming planes from *Franklin* and *Enterprise*. Other than making a great roar, even these guns did little to slow or deter the attackers.

By then, *Musashi* had taken another torpedo and was beginning to list.

Zero plunges into the water

Bombs and torpedoes rend the giant *Musashi*

She dropped out of formation, even though Kurita ordered the fleet to slow to 22 knots. More bombs and torpedoes hit the battleship, so that by 3:20 P.M. she could make only six knots. Emergency pumping and damage control had no effect on the ship, even when Kurita ordered her beached on the nearest island so that she could become a land battery.

Finally, about 7 P.M., the wounded captain of *Musashi* ordered his executive officer to abandon ship. By that time *Musashi* had taken 17 bomb and 19 torpedo hits and was likely to sink at any moment. Suddenly she began to roll on her side. The survivors of the air attacks scrambled to stay aboard by running over the razor-sharp barnacles on the hull until they could get in position to leap clear. Many never made it. Others, who did get clear of the ship, drowned in the hot oil that covered the surface of the sea or were sucked down by the boiling vortex formed when *Musashi* plunged, bow first, into the depths. Some 1,100 men went down with the great ship, about half her crew. Those who survived were subsequently picked up by Kurita's undamaged destroyers.

After the loss of *Musashi* and his other heavy combatants, Kurita decided to retire westward, hoping that darkness would protect him from further air attacks. Later, he again changed course and headed eastward for San Bernardino Strait and the amphibious forces at Leyte.

While Admiral Halsey monitored the air action over Kurita's force, he pondered where the Japanese carriers were. He knew that their carrier fleet had survived the action off Saipan and he could not believe that the enemy would commit its surface heavies without also bringing its carriers into the action.

This doubt concerning the whereabouts of Ozawa's Northern Force was soon resolved. Earlier, Ozawa had tried to draw Halsey's attention northward on purpose, because his job was to be the bait. The Japanese admiral wanted to divert Halsey and his carriers away from Leyte northward, so that the beachhead would be left uncovered. With the flanks of the assault forces uncovered, the Center and Southern Forces would be able to blast the defenseless transports with their big guns.

Late in the afternoon of 24 October, scouts from Task Force 38 found the Northern Force only 190 miles away. Halsey then had to choose be-

40-mm gun crew in action

tween three alternatives. One was to stay put and play a defensive role guarding the beachhead. Another was to divide his force—go after Ozawa with his carriers while leaving some of his battleships, cruisers and destroyers (organized as Task Force 34) behind to cover Kinkaid's flank. Or, finally, he could leave San Bernardino Strait unguarded and go after the Northern Force with his whole fleet.

In his operational plan for Leyte, Admiral Nimitz had directed Halsey to "cover and support forces of the Southwest Pacific [basically, Seventh Fleet and its amphibious shipping]," but he had also added these instructions for the Commander, Third Fleet: "In case opportunity for destruction of major portion of the enemy fleet offer or can be created, such destruction becomes the primary task." On the basis of these somewhat ambiguous orders—cover the invasion force but try to destroy the enemy fleet—Halsey decided to go after Ozawa with all his ships, carriers, battleships, cruisers and destroyers. "My job," he later wrote, "was offensive, to strike with the Third Fleet."

At the time Halsey chose to go north after the Japanese carriers and uncover the Leyte beachhead, there seemed to be strong justification for the move. Kurita and the Center Force had suffered serious losses and appeared to be retiring westward. The Southern Force was still a potential threat, but Halsey knew that Rear Admiral Jesse B. Oldendorf's force, guarding Surigao Strait, had both knowledge of the advancing enemy force and the firepower to deal with it.

In this latter surmise, Halsey was subsequently proven correct. Oldendorf's 6 old battleships, 4 heavy and 4 light cruisers and 21 destroyers nearly annihilated Nishimura's force in a night gunnery action in the early morning hours of 25 October. Nishimura lost two battleships and a heavy cruiser sunk and several destroyers damaged. Admiral Shima, who realized he was heading for a trap when he saw what had happened to Nishimura's van, wisely withdrew to the westward, having suffered only minor damage to his ships.

Halsey's three task groups of carriers and escorts shaped a course toward Ozawa's Northern Force at 25 knots. Once he learned that Halsey had grabbed his bait, Ozawa reversed course and started to withdraw northward. He also radioed Kurita that his part of the Japanese plan had worked. This message, however, was never received by the commander of the Center Force.

When search planes from Task Force 38 located the Northern Force shortly after 7 A.M. on 25 October, Admiral Mitscher ordered his air strike groups to "get the carriers." Immediately 180 planes flew off the American flight decks and headed north.

The Northern Force consisted of one heavy and three light carriers, two battleships that had been converted to carriers, three light cruisers and eight destroyers. Other than their combined antiaircraft fire, they could offer only about a dozen fighters in opposition to Mitscher's air armada. The Northern Force was essentially a hollow shell. Thus the bombers and torpedo planes from Task Force 38 had little difficulty getting through the enemy planes. They quickly sank a destroyer, hit the light carriers *Zuiho* and *Chitose* and torpedoed the fast carrier *Zuikaku*, the sole surviving carrier from the attack on Pearl Harbor. *Chitose* then took a torpedo hit below the waterline and sank.

A second air strike around 10 A.M. did more damage. It slowed the cruiser *Tama* and set the light carrier *Chiyoda* afire. Three torpedoes and several bombs hit *Zuikaku*, sending her to the bottom. The light carrier *Zuiho* was also hit, but good damage control put out the fires. In subsequent air strikes that afternoon, *Zuiho* took about a dozen bomb hits and two torpedoes, which eventually finished her off.

The destruction of Ozawa's Northern Force was not carried out without loss to the Americans. The antiaircraft fire from the gunships was intense, and some of the Japanese fighter planes managed to shoot down a few attackers. One of the fighter pilots who had to bail out as a result of repeated hits from a Japanese Zero was Ensign George Denby. In his afteraction report, Denby told how he had had trouble with his parachute once he had jumped clear of his plane and then was strafed momentarily by an enemy fighter.

After he hit the water, Denby did what he could to untangle himself from the parachute. He discovered, however, that he was in real trouble. He had lost his life raft when his chute opened. His Mae West had a rip in it, which meant that he had to keep it inflated by blowing into it. In addition, the damaged life jacket would not support his head; he had to swim constantly to stay afloat.

Then the young ensign found he had another problem—sharks. The action report describes his situation in this manner:

"As he swam, his socks gradually worked off, leaving his bare feet as a lure for sharks, which promptly put in an appearance. A number of them, always 4 or more, 4–5 feet long, stayed with him continuously but did not bother him unless he stopped kicking. However, when he stopped to rest for a moment one of them would make a pass at him and one of them actually grabbed the calf of his left leg, leaving tooth marks."

Finally, after he had been in the water nearly two hours, a friendly

143

destroyer found Denby and picked him up, but not before its propeller wash forced him under twice, nearly drowning him. The ship had to put a swimmer in the water who passed a line under the pilot's arms so that he could be hauled aboard, as the report concluded, "considerably the worse for wear."

While Mitscher's pilots were busy dealing with the Japanese Northern Force, Kurita's Center Force unexpectedly turned up east of the island of Samar, just north of Leyte Gulf. Kurita had reversed course once more during the night and headed for his original destination with 4 battleships, 6 heavy and 2 light cruisers and 11 destroyers. At sunrise the Japanese, who lacked radar, saw the masts and hulls of Kinkaid's supporting force of 6 escort carriers, 3 destroyers and 4 destroyer escorts. However, they thought they were seeing Halsey's Third Fleet, which was in fact 300 miles to the north.

Three groups of escort carriers and destroyers, designated Taffy 1, 2 and 3, were all that stood between Kurita's *Yamato* and other big guns and MacArthur's amphibious forces on the beach at Leyte. Kurita ordered "General Attack" at 6:58 A.M., and the ships opened fire on the Americans, who were taken completely by surprise.

The escort carriers immediately turned tail at flank speed (18 knots) because they were simply no match for the 14-, 16- and 18-inch guns of Kurita's force. In desperation, they put every plane into the air as they headed downwind, hoping that their Hellcats and Avengers could disrupt the enemy fire and cause some damage of their own. The destroyers, in the meantime, tried to hide the escort carriers with smoke screens and then turned and attacked the enemy.

The destroyer *Johnston* hit the heavy cruiser *Kumano* with a torpedo, putting her out of action. Other torpedoes hit the heavy cruisers *Chokai* and *Chikuma*. A bomb from one of the escort carriers' planes hit another heavy cruiser. Other torpedoes, fired at *Yamato,* forced the Japanese to turn away, blunting their attack to some degree.

While the light American ships—the escort carriers and destroyers— were doing their heroic best to hold off the Japanese, Kinkaid was trying to locate Halsey, who he thought was guarding Leyte with his big-gun ships in Task Force 34. A surprised Kinkaid soon learned that Halsey was attacking Ozawa far to the north. The defenders at Leyte could not expect immediate help from the fast carriers or the battleships.

Although Halsey immediately detached his battleships and cruisers and one carrier group from Task Force 38 and headed south as fast as possible once he realized the danger at Leyte, he did not arrive in the vicinity of

Kamikaze hit ignites a carrier's flight deck

San Bernardino Strait until around midnight. By that time the action off Samar Island was all over.

Despite all the counter fire and air attacks on the Japanese force, Kurita's gunners soon began to get the range on the American ships. They hit the destroyer *Hoel* with over 40 shells. Soon the destroyer escort *Sam-*

uel B. Roberts was sunk by 14-inch cruiser fire. The damaged *Johnston* continued to attack aggressively, but she too could not withstand repeat hits. Her surviving senior officer described her under the attack as being "like a puppy being smacked by a truck."

The escort carriers also began to take hits. One, *Gambier Bay*, cap-

Across the water smoke rolls from the *Suwannee*

sized and sank shortly after 9 A.M. Despite having sunk these ships, the Japanese were not closing in on Leyte. Attacks by all the American aircraft that were locally available were supplementing the harrassment by the destoyers. These air attacks were continuous, and pilots who had expended their ammunition even made dry runs on enemy ships to divert their fire.

In the confusion of the battle, Kurita was unable to determine what was happening to his forces. The American planes had downed *Yamato's* last two scout planes, and his radiotelephone was not working. He had to guess at the results of his van's attack on the escort carriers. Judging that the smoke up ahead meant that the American forces had escaped before being annihilated, he ordered his ships to head north at 20 knots shortly after 9 A.M. Upon receipt of this order, two Japanese heavy cruisers immediately reversed course and broke off action with the carriers at nearly point-blank range. Incredibly, the American task unit of escort carriers and destroyers was saved from further damage and destruction as a result of Kurita's uncertainty about the tactical situation.

Following the withdrawal of the Japanese Center Force toward San Bernardino Strait, the action off Leyte came to a close, but the hazards of naval operations on 25 October were not over. Six Japanese planes took off from an airfield with one goal: to crash into American ships. These were the planes of the recently organized *Kamikaze* ("Divine Wind") Special Attack Corps. They, too, found the escort carriers off Leyte. Two of the suicide planes hit the carriers *Suwanee* and *Santee*, tearing great holes in their flight and hangar decks but not sinking them. Later other kamikazes hit the escort carriers *Kitkun Bay*, *Kalinin Bay* and *St. Lô*. The last of these carriers, *St. Lô*, caught fire when the crashing airplane detonated bombs and torpedoes on the hangar deck. The fires set off more explosions nearly blowing the ship apart. She sank around noon.

The use of kamikazes indicated that the Japanese had expended all their conventional weapons—aircraft, battleships and carriers—on the enemy, and that none of these had stopped the Americans' advance. Clawing desperately at any chance to turn defeat into victory, they were ready to try these deliberate suicide attacks in the hope that they might achieve what had not been possible with their other weapons.

The U.S. Navy and its allied forces would have to face this new test in the campaigns ahead. The advance toward the Home Islands meant that Japanese resistance would be even tougher and more determined than before. The prospects for eventual victory over Japan following the Battle of Leyte Gulf were bright, but the course that the Allies would have to shape toward that victory was beset by a new danger.

10. The Last Battles

Although the first organized kamikaze attacks on the U.S. fleet occurred on 25 October 1944 at Leyte Gulf, this was not the first time that Japanese pilots had tried to crash American warships in a premeditated manner. Throughout the war pilots on both sides had sometimes sought to achieve some final blow against the enemy by diving a hopelessly crippled plane into an enemy carrier or warship. These deliberate crashes usually resulted spontaneously from combat damage to the plane or mortal wounds to the pilot. Japanese fighter pilot Saburo Sakai tells in his autobiography how he took part in the first premeditated suicide attack in early July 1944. At that time he was flying from a base on Iwo Jima. The U.S. Navy's Task Force 58 had just crippled the Japanese fleet in the Marianas Turkey Shoot. According to Sakai, his wing commander on Iwo Jima decided that his pilots must strike back at the enemy in the only way possible: suicide attacks. The commander, Captain Kanzo Miura, gave his 17 pilots this order:

"Individual attacks must be forgotten. You cannot strike your targets as one man alone. You must maintain a tight group of planes. You must fight your way

149

through the interceptors, and you must dive against the enemy carriers together! Dive—along with your torpedoes and your lives and souls!"

Sakai goes on to explain that unlike kamikaze pilots who later volunteered for their one-way missions, he and his fellow pilots on Iwo Jima were ordered to crash the enemy ships deliberately. For him there was a great difference between being prepared to die in battle should death come and being prepared to kill oneself deliberately. Sakai and his fellow pilots took off on their suicide mission, but he survived because a defensive patrol of Hellcats broke up their attack 50 miles from the carriers. Sakai realized that he would never get close enough to get a chance to crash a carrier at this extreme range. Hence he returned to Iwo Jima, some 400 miles distant, rather than waste his life in a needless way.

The Special Attack Corps or *Kamikaze Tokubetsu Kogekitai* that originated in the Japanese Navy's First Air Fleet on the Philippines was born from the same desire to attack the enemy that had motivated Sakai's commanding officer. Vice Admiral Takijiro Onishi, who as commander of the First Air Fleet used this weapon at Leyte, did not have to order his men to crash their planes into the American ships. That was unnecessary. They wanted to make this supreme sacrifice for their country.

The idea of the "divine wind" was taken from an actual event in Japan's long history. Twice Kublai Khan, the great Mongol leader and warrior, had tried to invade the island of Kyushu in the 13th century, but both times powerful typhoons had wrecked the invasion force and protected Japan. Onishi hoped that his pilots could do the same against the Fast Carrier Task Force. By the fall of 1944, most Japanese military leaders had recognized that orthodox methods of air attack could not crack the fighter and antiaircraft defenses of the American fleet. Thus they turned to the kamikazes.

Captain Rikibei Inoguchi, who was Admiral Onishi's chief of staff in the Philippines, summarized the reasoning of those who supported the use of kamikazes:

"We must give our lives to the Emperor and [the] Country, this is our inborn feeling. I am afraid [Americans] cannot understand it well, as you may call it desperate or foolish. We Japanese base our lives on obedience to Emperor and Country. On the other hand, we wish for the best place in death, according to Bushido [the Japanese warrior code]. Kamikaze originates from these feelings."

Captain Inoguchi went on to explain that no special preparations were necessary with the kamikazes. Volunteer pilots underwent a brief period of training, usually no more than 300 and sometimes as little as 100 hours in the simplest types of aircraft, before being sent out on their one-way missions.

Suicide pilots simply did not need elaborate training. Normally a reconnaissance plane would locate the enemy force to be attacked. Then a kamikaze unit would take off escorted by experienced pilots in fighter planes. Once the kamikazes reached the American ships, they would try to carry out their mission of death. The fighter pilots would observe the results and report to headquarters. Inoguchi estimated that one-sixth of all the kamikazes used in the Philippine campaign hit their targets and that in the subsequent battle of Okinawa about one-ninth of the suicide planes succeeded in crashing an enemy target.

Following their first use in the Battle for Leyte Gulf, the kamikazes repeatedly struck Admiral Halsey's Third Fleet. When the fleet finally withdrew to Ulithi in late November for resupply and rest from three months of nearly continuous combat operations, six carriers had been damaged by these suicide attacks.

The break in combat operations that Third Fleet enjoyed at Ulithi did not last long, because Halsey's ships were needed to cover MacArthur's further amphibious operations. Once Task Force 38 had reached its operating area off the Philippines, Vice Admiral John S. McCain, now commander of Task Force 38, adopted a radical procedure for coping with the kamikazes. His planes flew continuous missions over the Japanese airfields in an effort to keep the kamikazes grounded or to shoot them down before they could get to the fleet. He called this operation the "Big Blue Blanket." McCain also reduced the number of dive-bombers on his fast carriers to less than half and more than doubled his fighters. In addition, he had his Hellcat and Corsair fighters modified to carry 2,000 pounds of bombs so that they were dual-purpose aircraft.

By this time, Marine aviators had begun training to fly off carriers for close-support missions and defense against kamikazes. Eventually they were embarked on four escort carriers—*Block Island, Gilbert Islands, Cape Gloucester* and *Vella Gulf*—for the landing operations in 1945, particularly the expected assault on the Japanese Home Islands.

Despite McCain's changes in his aircraft and the blanket technique for keeping the suicide planes down, the Third Fleet did not escape undamaged from this foray to the Philippines. But the damage it sustained, however, resulted from another kind of enemy—real typhoons. Owing to sketchy weather reporting, Halsey received very late notification that a severe typhoon, labeled Cobra, was in his vicinity. His ships were caught in the middle of it.

151

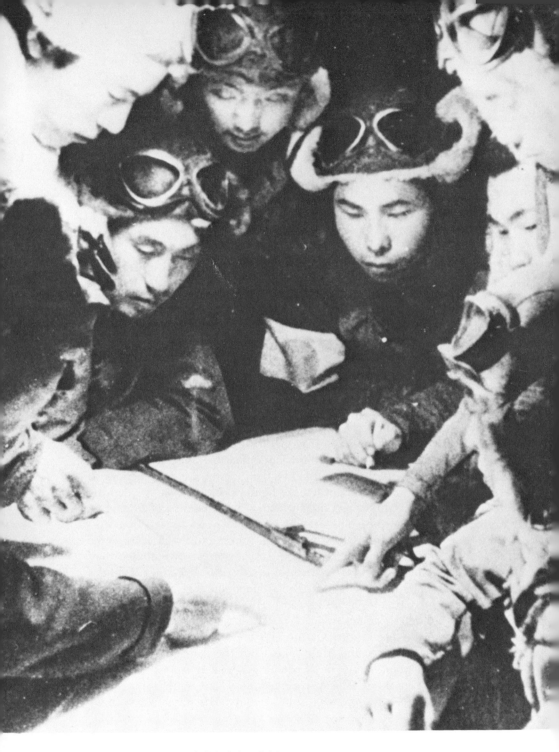

Kamikaze pilots are briefed the night
before a sortie

Suicide pilot receives his orders

The crews of Third Fleet ships realized they were in the presence of a typhoon on 18 December, when visibility dropped to near zero, the winds reached 75 miles per hour with gusts as high as 120 miles per hour and the seas became mountainously high. Smaller vessels, such as destroyers, reported rolling 70 degrees at times. The winds and seas tore carrier aircraft from their moorings on deck and swept them overboard or threw them across the hangar decks, often starting dangerous fires. The fleet lost 186 aircraft from storm damage.

Unable to keep formation, course or speed, many of Halsey's ships simply tried to manage in the storm as best they could. In the book *Halsey's Typhoons*, Lieutenant Robert J. Lauer, who was on the light carrier *San Jacinto*, described what happened on his ship:

> "It was a terrifying sight to watch the gigantic breakers on the crest of the seas looming up, sometimes as much as 30 degrees above the horizontal, as the ship slowly rolled through 40 degrees or more. It would have been suicide to venture onto the flight deck."

On the hangar deck, some of *San Jacinto*'s planes broke loose. The entire deck was "a mass of flying carnage threatening sure death to anyone who dared enter onto it." Soon it was covered with gasoline and oil. A spark suddenly ignited these combustibles. Fortunately, the alert carrier men could turn on the sprinkling system on the hangar deck and they could spray chemical foam on the fires from the openings on the adjacent catwalks. But, as Lieutenant Lauer explained, the water and foam "combined with the torrential rain and seawater from openings punctured in the sides soon produced a virtual flooding of the hangar deck. Then machine gun ammunition from the planes began to go off, fired by the flames and by being struck with the flying debris."

When *San Jacinto* finally escaped the typhoon and reached Ulithi, her crew members were convinced they would have to be sent back to the West Coast for repairs. However, the engineers on the repair ship *Hector* at Ulithi evaluated the damage differently. They estimated that they could have the carrier ready for action in 10 days' time.

Besides the *San Jacinto*, the light carriers *Monterey* and *Cowpens* and the destroyers and destroyer escorts *Hickox*, *Dyson*, *Buchanan* and *Laws* suffered heavy damage. Three destroyers—*Hull*, *Monaghan* and *Spence*—were low in fuel when they were caught in the storm, and they were unable to ballast their fuel tanks fully with sea water to provide greater stability in the mountainous seas. All three capsized at the peak of the storm's fury and sank. A total of 80 men, of whom only six were from *Spence*, were rescued by the other ships in the Third Fleet; 790 lives were lost in the typhoon. This battering from Typhoon Cobra damaged Halsey's ships as much as a major battle might have.

The Fast Carrier Task Force returned to combat with the Japanese in early January 1945 in support of MacArthur's forces at Lingayen Gulf, on the west coast of Luzon. Once more the kamikazes dealt destruction to the American fleet, sinking the escort carrier *Ommaney Bay* and severely damaging the escort carriers *Manila Bay* and *Kitkun Bay*, the cruisers *Louisville* and *Australia* and three minesweepers.

As MacArthur's troops slowly gained a foothold on Luzon and pushed ahead toward Manila, Halsey was able to return to Ulithi. There he turned over command to Admirals Spruance and Mitscher, and the Third Fleet once again became the Fifth Fleet. While Halsey and McCain had been fighting the Japanese and Typhoon Cobra, Spruance and Mitscher had been planning for their next mission—the assault on Iwo Jima.

Beginning in November 1944, B-29 Superfortresses of the Army Air Forces had been flying bombing raids from Saipan to Tokyo. This 3,000-mile round-trip flight had limited the big bombers to carrying only three tons of explosives instead of a possible 10. And since no fighters could fly such a distance as escorts, the B-29s had to drop their bombs from around 28,000 feet, which meant they were not very precise in hitting their targets. In addition, Japanese bases in the Bonin and Volcano Islands, which lie between the Marianas and Japan, not only alerted Tokyo to the approach of each raid but also sent up fighters to attack the B-29s. The capture of one of the islands in the Bonin-Volcano group would put an end to this harassment from the Japanese, and it would provide a base for fighter cover for the B-29s and a way station for damaged bombers en route home. Iwo Jima, which is part of the Volcanoes, was quickly selected as the target island for capture because it had the best airfields.

On D-day, 19 February 1945, eight battalions of marines hit the beach of volcanic ash on Iwo Jima. Although the invaders suffered heavy losses from the steady Japanese defensive fire, they had soon seized a foothold. By nightfall 30,000 marines were established on the island; 2,400 had already become casualties.

While the marines were engaged in the bitter fighting on Iwo Jima, Task Force 58 steamed close to the shore with its planes flying strikes against enemy gun emplacements or bombing, strafing and rocketing other targets. Although there was no enemy air opposition and antiaircraft fire was minimal, Japanese targets were still hard to hit because most of the enemy positions were in well-protected caves.

The Japanese fought back against these strikes with air attacks on the

Photos show an F6F burning on the deck of *Lexington*. In the second picture the pilot escapes the flames

carriers, usually made late in the afternoon or at night. On 21 February some 20 kamikazes attacked the American ships, damaging the escort carriers *Lunga Point* and *Bismarck Sea*. The fires that the suicide planes started on *Bismarck Sea* set off so much antiaircraft ammunition that the crew was forced to abandon the ship before she sank. Four enemy aircraft and two bombs also hit the fast carrier *Saratoga*, setting her afire and blasting a large underwater hole in her hull. Skillful damage control and firefighting parties saved the ship, but the damage was so extensive that she was ordered to return to the West Coast for repairs. She suffered 110 killed and 180 wounded from this kamikaze attack.

When not operating in support of the marines on Iwo Jima, the planes of Task Force 58 carried out strikes over Japan. The first raids on the Home Islands had taken place on 16 and 17 February. Carrier-based planes hit Tokyo on 25 February in coordination with a bombing run by more than 200 B-29s from the Marianas. Fighter opposition over the Japanese capital was weak, although the antiaircraft fire was intense.

The "jeep"—escort—carriers that were operating off Iwo Jima provided tireless support to the forces ashore during the month of bloody fighting it took the marines to secure the island. Between 16 February and 11 March, aircraft from the escort carriers flew 8,800 sorties against enemy gun positions, pillboxes, supply dumps and troop concentrations. The jeeps also carried out antisubmarine patrols and were credited with one possible sinking and with damaging three other enemy subs.

By 26 March, Iwo Jima was securely in the hands of U.S. forces. It could now serve as a base, 660 miles from Tokyo, where crippled B-29s from Saipan could find help when they were short of fuel or otherwise in trouble. Consequently, more lives of B-29 pilots and aircrew members were saved by the forces on Iwo Jima in the remaining months of the war than had been lost in the capturing of the island.

Once Iwo Jima was taken, Task Force 58 returned to Ulithi to rest and resupply before the next amphibious operation, the assault on Okinawa. The main landings were scheduled for 1 April. Okinawa, which is part of the Ryukyu Islands south of Japan proper, was the last island that Allied planners expected to take before the assault on the Home Islands, which was scheduled to begin in November 1945 with landings on Kyushu.

For the Okinawa campaign, Admiral Spruance's Fifth Fleet included four fast carrier task groups in Task Force 58 and one fast carrier task group from the Royal Navy, designated Task Force 57.

Under the command of Rear Admiral Sir Philip Vian, Task Force 57 comprised 4 fast carriers—*Illustrious, Indomitable, Indefatigable* and *Victorious*—and their escorts—2 battleships, 5 cruisers and 10 destroyers. The

Suicide pilot in a Zero tries to crash the USS
Missouri—a near miss

Fleet Air Arm on the carriers included the usual British aircraft, particularly the Fairey Firefly, as well as American planes.

Prior to joining Spruance's Fifth Fleet, the British Pacific Fleet carried out three raids on Japanese oil refineries in Sumatra in an attempt to cut down the supply of aviation fuel that was reaching Japan. By the time Task Force 57 took station south and west of Okinawa to protect the Allied assault forces from Japanese airfields on Taiwan, it was a seasoned fast carrier task force.

When the landings began on Okinawa on 1 April, the Fifth Fleet included 1,300 ships carrying 182,000 troops under the command of Lieutenant General Simon Bolivar Buckner, Jr., USA. Although the Japanese had about 100,000 defenders on the island, the initial landings were made without difficulty or great opposition because once again the Japanese had decided to rely upon defense in depth. They had withdrawn from the beaches to natural strongpoints formed by the steep hills and narrow ravines on the island. Lieutenant General Mitsuru Ushijima, the Japanese commander on Okinawa, planned to fight a war of attrition in which the American land and naval forces would be exposed to attack by Japanese air power, particularly kamikazes.

Since the American soldiers and marines on Okinawa would have to take each Japanese strongpoint individually, the fast carriers of Task Force 58 stayed close to the island—generally to the northeast, so that they would be in position to protect against any attacks from Japan itself. The fighting ashore was extremely difficult because of the complex of fortified positions and the network of caves that the Japanese had dug. Thus Army commanders occasionally requested that planes from Task Force 58 bomb an enemy cave even though it might be only 50 yards from positions held by American soldiers.

As part of his defense against kamikaze attacks during these operations near Okinawa, Admiral Mitscher stationed a number of radar picket destroyers north of the island in the direction of Japan. Despite these precautions, the kamikazes hit Fifth Fleet ships with regularity. By 5 April the suicide pilots had damaged 39 naval vessels, including Admiral Spruance's flagship, the cruiser *Indianapolis*. But the first large, general suicide attack did not come until 6 April, when 355 kamikazes swarmed over Task Force 58.

Combat air patrols and accurate antiaircraft fire protected the carriers from this aerial assault, but the radar picket destroyers suffered greatly, two of them being sunk. The antiaircraft fire from the task force was so intense that falling shell fragments caused 38 American casualties. Twenty-two ships suffered some degree of damage from the attack.

160

Even before this mass attack, Task Force 58 had taken significant damage from the suicide planes during preliminary air strikes in March. While attacking Japanese bases on Kyushu, the kamikazes had hit the fast carriers *Yorktown, Enterprise, Intrepid* and *Wasp*. A fifth fast carrier, the *Franklin,* had also taken a 500-pound bomb which had ignited the fuel and ammunition in the planes on her deck, setting off tremendous explosions. More than 800 members of her crew died in these blasts. The commander of the task group to which *Franklin* was assigned reported to Mitscher that the carrier would have to be abandoned. But Captain Leslie Gehres, skipper of the *Franklin,* disagreed. He called Mitscher over the voice radio (TBS) and said, "This is the commanding officer of the *Franklin.* You save us from the Japs and we'll save this ship." Mitscher then told his chief of staff, Captain Arleigh Burke, "You tell him we'll save him." With that, Mitscher ordered the task force to retire southward, covering the *Franklin.* Her crew kept the carrier afloat and eventually she returned to the United States under her own power for extensive repairs.

On 21 March the Japanese had also unveiled another form of suicide weapon in attacks on Task Force 58. This was the Ohka (Cherry Blossom) piloted bomb. Manned by volunteers, these winged, rocket-propelled bombs were released from the underside of a conventional Betty bomber. Steered by the pilot, they then glided toward a target. About 20 feet long, having a wingspan of more than 16 feet, the Ohka bomb carried 2,640 pounds of explosive in its nose section. Although the Americans dubbed them the "Baka" bombs, using the Japanese word meaning "foolish" or "stupid," no one would want to fool with them once launched, because their rockets could propel them at speeds between 575 and 650 miles an hour. They were extremely difficult to shoot down with fighters or antiaircraft fire.

In addition to the kamikazes and the Ohka bombs, the Japanese launched a third kind of suicide mission. On 6 April the superbattleship *Yamato,* the light cruiser *Yahagi* and eight destroyers sortied from the Inland Sea with only 2,500 tons of fuel oil, just enough to get them to Okinawa. Once there, they planned to beach their ships and shell the American ground forces until they had expended all their ammunition or were destroyed.

Shortly after these last remnants of the once-proud Japanese fleet had entered the Pacific Ocean, a U.S. submarine reported their movements to Admiral Spruance. Once informed of the movements of *Yamato,* Spruance ordered Mitscher to move his carriers northward and launch his planes for the attack. Around noon on 7 April, aircraft from Task Force 58 began their attack on *Yamato* and her escorts. Within 10 minutes the superbattleship

USS Franklin: ''We'll save this ship''

Superbattleship *Yamato*

had taken two bomb hits and a torpedo, while one destroyer was sunk and *Yahagi* severely damaged. The carrier planes attacked in pairs or in threes from all directions against inadequate antiaircraft fire. By 2 P.M. *Yamato* had taken eight torpedo hits, was listing and had lost steering control. More torpedoes hit her, increasing the list to 35 degrees. One survivor of *Yamato*'s last sortie, Ensign Mitsuru Yoshida, has left an account of what it was like in the last moments on the superbattleship:

> "I could hear the Captain vainly shouting, "Hold on, men! Hold on, men!" . . . I heard the executive officer report . . . "Correction of listing hopeless!" . . . The deck was nearly vertical and *Yamato*'s battle flag was almost touching the billowing waves . . . Shells of the big guns skidded and bumped across the deck of the ammunition room, crashing against the bulkhead and kindling the first of a series of explosions. [At 2:43 P.M.] the ship slid under completely [followed by] the blast, rumble, and shock of compartments bursting from air pressure and exploding magazines already submerged."

The light cruiser *Yahagi* followed *Yamato* to the bottom of the Pacific after she took a total of 12 bomb and seven torpedo hits. Four of the destroyers were also sunk; the others, although damaged, were able to return to Japan.

The Japanese Special Surface Attack Force, as the *Yamato* group was

164

called, lost not only most of its ships but also 3,655 officers and men. Only 269 men from *Yamato* survived the attack. American losses in planes were light, about 15, with 84 men lost in the air attack and as a result of a kamikaze attack on the carrier *Hancock* (in which 43 men were killed).

The Japanese and their kamikazes were not winning their battle with Task Force 58, but on 11 April they staged another massive attack on the carriers. One Japanese Judy headed for *Enterprise* from dead astern, the carrier's most vulnerable spot. The ship's antiaircraft poured shells into the plane, but it kept coming. As Edward Stafford describes it, the gunners on the ship's port quarter knew that

Kamikazes wreaked havoc off Okinawa

"their only chance was to take his plane apart with their bullets before it reached them. They stuck to their weapons, hammering the Judy until it filled the world before them, hit and disintegrated in a roar and blast and sudden silence like the end of the earth. A seaman was blown overboard and two more fell with broken legs and arms. The Judy's wing had hit between the two [gun] mounts. His engine dished in the hull plating, and his bomb grazed the ship's side and detonated under the turn of the bilge, shaking her as a terrier shakes a snake."

As in the past, expert damage control and fire fighting helped keep the Big E going. But others, like *Intrepid*, were not so fortunate. Two kamikazes dove on her simultaneously. Her gunners shot one down but the other hit the flight deck aft, ripping a hole 12 by 14 feet in the deck, destroying 40 aircraft and killing nine men and wounding 40 others.

Day after day in April and May, while Task Force 58 steamed off Okinawa, the kamikazes attacked the American ships. None were immune. Although the carriers were the major targets, the kamikazes also sank several picket destroyers. On the average, the task force's combat air patrol shot down 20 to 30 enemy planes each day.

On 17 April, for example, four pilots from Fighter Squadron 9 on *Yorktown*, led by Lieutenant Eugene A. Valencia, shot down at least 14 enemy planes and probably three more. Valencia alone had six confirmed victories in that mission. By the end of the war, Valencia's "mowing machine," as his fighter team was called, had tallied 50 enemy planes shot down and all four pilots were aces.

The Royal Navy's ships in Task Force 57 enjoyed no security from kamikaze attack. During one attack on HMS *Formidable* on 4 May, a suicide plane crossed the carrier from port to starboard and headed aft, apparently seeking a better attack angle on the ship. One observer, whose account appears in John Winton's anthology *The War at Sea*, vividly described what happened next:

Then the Jap came into sight again from behind the island, banking hard to close the ship over the starboard quarter . . . I had waited long enough and ran about fifteen yards forward to a hatch, down which I jumped in the company of a rather fat leading seaman. As we hit the deck an immense crash shook the ship. I gave it a second or two to subside, during which the light from above changed to bright orange, and ran up again.

It was a grim sight. A fire was blazing among wreckage close under the bridge, flames reached up the side of the island and clouds of black smoke billowed far above the ship . . . The deck was littered with debris, much of it on fire, and there was not a soul to be seen.

Despite the damage, the fires were quickly extinguished and repairs made. Unlike the American carriers, the British flattops had armored flight decks, which withstood the impact of the suicide planes much better than the light steel and wood of the American decks.

For nearly three months, the fast carriers operated in or near Okinawa in support of the ground forces, which slowly gained control of the island. During this time, the enemy made 1,900 kamikaze and 3,700 conventional sorties against the Americans. The damage caused by these attacks was extensive: 12 destroyers sunk and major repairs required on 10 battleships, 13 carriers, 5 cruisers and 67 destroyers. One of these kamikaze attacks finally damaged *Enterprise* enough to put her out of the war. A Zeke fighter dived down the carrier's forward elevator, exploding its bomb five decks below the place of entry. Although 13 men were killed and 68 wounded in the explosion, the body of the Japanese pilot, Chief Pilot Tomi Zai, survived the blast and fire. He was subsequently identified from the calling cards that were found undamaged in his pocket.

Finally, on 21 June, the U.S. Army command on Okinawa declared the island secured, even though mopping-up operations continued until the end of the month. With the fall of Okinawa, the planners in the Fifth Fleet expected that they would next be preparing for an assault on Japan. Thus the carriers began systematic air attacks on major Japanese military and industrial targets in conjunction with the B-29 raids.

At the conclusion of operations off Okinawa, the Halsey-McCain team once more took command of the fast carriers. Subsequently Halsey's Third Fleet steamed off the coast of Japan with impunity. The enemy hoarded their aircraft against the impending assault. But that assault never came. The dropping of the atomic bombs on Hiroshima and Nagasaki on 6 and 9 August, respectively, devastated those cities and hastened the Japanese efforts to obtain peace. The Third Fleet received its "cease fire" orders on 15 August. The carrier war with Japan was over. The carrier victory had been won.

The fast carriers of the U.S. Navy had shown how aircraft could go to sea and provide the mobility and offensive power necessary to win control of an ocean. In World War II, the particular strength of the Fast Carrier Task Force, according to Vice Admiral Jinsaburo Ozawa, was "in the use of radar, [the] interception of radio messages, and [the] intercept[ion] by radar of Japanese air attacks which [the Americans] could catch and destroy . . . whenever they want[ed] to."

Although the U.S. Navy had established its dominance with the fast carriers, it found after the war that it had many more flattops than it needed or wanted. Many, like *Enterprise*, eventually were cut up and sold for scrap in the 1950s, but a few survived into the 1960s, as a result of modernization programs, and saw action off Vietnam. Even though the carriers of World War II are nearly all gone, their memory endures either in the accounts of the battles they fought or in the physical presence of new fast

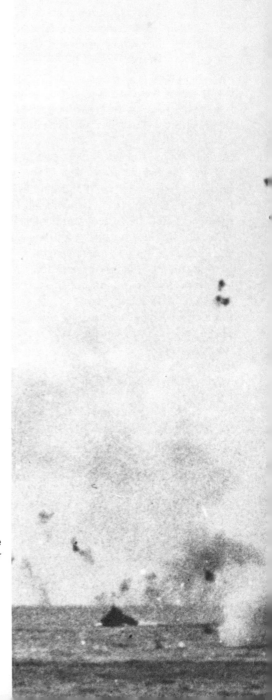

Enterprise—six times claimed sunk, she survives the war

carriers bearing familiar names, such as the nuclear-powered *Enterprise,* which have demonstrated once again the mobility and vast striking power provided by an air navy.

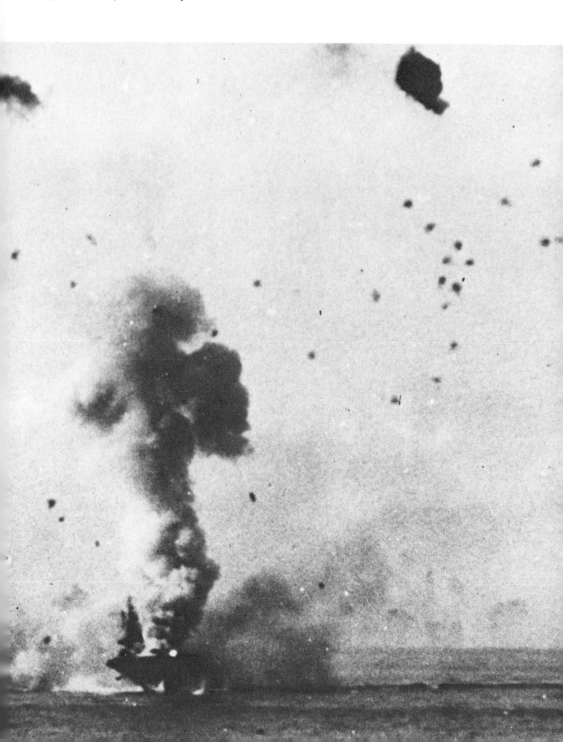

In Context

In *Carrier Victory* we have followed American forces in the Pacific from the shock of Pearl Harbor through the struggle against the kamikazes off Okinawa. The operations described here were some of the most original and daring in the history of warfare.

But we need to be reminded that, for much of the world, the war had begun long before the Japanese attacked the United States. Some historians have argued (and with good reason) that the summer of 1937, when the smoldering situation in China erupted into flame and the Sino-Japanese war was on, should be regarded as the beginning of World War II. The usual date for the outbreak of the war, however, is 1 September 1939, when at dawn the Germany of Adolf Hitler launched its invasion of Poland.

It was a quick, victorious campaign for the German armies. And in 1940, while Japan pursued her goals in China, the Germans swept through western Europe in an amazing march of conquest: Denmark, Norway, the Netherlands, Luxembourg, Belgium and, to the world's shock, France. The Führer seemed all-conquering. But his remaining foe, Britain, was an island protected by a navy and an air force. The German armies could not cross water, unless they were ferried over it in boats and protected by air superiority. The Battle of Britain, fought in the summer of 1940, was waged to determine control of the air over England. The German Luftwaffe lost—and the war in Europe and Africa went on.

In 1941 Hitler turned east again, sending his armies into the Soviet Union on 22 June. Britain and the still-neutral United States sprang to Russia's aid with lend-lease munitions and supplies. At the same time, President Roosevelt and his advisers were viewing Japan's attempts to establish the "greater East Asia Co-Prosperity Sphere"—the extension of the Japanese Empire to Burma, Indochina, Malaya and the Netherlands East Indies—with deep concern.

The Axis partners—Germany, Italy and Japan—seemed to be riding the wave of victory as 1941 unfolded. But the great German invasion of the Soviet Union was stopped at the gates of Moscow, and in this same December came the Japanese attack on Pearl Harbor, bringing the United States into alliance with Britain and Russia against the Axis.

Even though it was a Japanese move that had propelled the Americans into the war, they adhered to previously drawn-up plans that called for the main initial effort to be made against Germany, the most powerful member of the Axis coalition. But, as we have seen in *Carrier Victory*, adoption of this strategy did not mean that nothing happened in the Pacific. The early American victories recounted in this book were some of the most important Allied triumphs of the war—particularly Midway, one of the truly decisive battles of the entire global struggle.

While the new kind of carrier warfare was evolving in the Pacific, on the other side of the world the Allies were taking the fight to the Axis on land and in the air. In the fall of 1942 the Anglo-Americans landed in Northwest Africa; they moved eastward to link up with British forces moving from Egypt. Having defeated the Germans in Africa, the Allied armies invaded Sicily, then Italy. In 1944 came the landings in Normandy, as the Soviets drove the Germans back from the east. Meanwhile a great Allied air offensive was demolishing Germany's cities (see the Men and Battle book *The Men Who Bombed the Reich*). The war in Europe did not end in 1944, as many had hoped, but the outcome could not be long delayed. In early May 1945 Nazi Germany was finished.

Even though American—and now British—carrier forces had become supreme in the Pacific, Allied commanders feared that Japan would go on fighting until bested in a bloody invasion. The last major operation of the war is described in *Okinawa: The Great Island Battle*, another Men and Battle book. There was an American saying at the time, "Golden Gate by forty-eight." But the dropping of the two atomic bombs changed the picture with dramatic suddenness. The old era of warfare was over.

For Further Reading

ADAMSON, HANS CHRISTIAN, and KOSCO, GEORGE FRANCIS. *Halsey's Typhoons: A Firsthand Account of how Two Typhoons, More Powerful than the Japanese, Dealt Death and Destruction to Admiral Halsey's Third Fleet.* New York: Crown, 1967.
George Kosco was Admiral Halsey's meteorologist in late 1944 and early 1945 and he and Adamson provide an extensive account of the damage two typhoons did to the Third Fleet.

ANDRIEU D'ALBAS, EMMANUEL MARIE AUGUSTE. *Death of a Navy: Japanese Naval Action in World War II.* Translated by Anthony Ribbon. New York: Devin-Adair, 1957.
A history of the naval war in the Pacific with particular attention to the role of the Japanese navy, its strengths and weaknesses, based on research in Allied and Japanese documents.

BROWN, DAVID. *Carrier Operations in World War II.* 2 vols. Annapolis: U.S. Naval Institute, 1974.
An operational history.
Vol. 1: Covers British naval aviation in World War II and the development of the Fleet Air Arm (FAA)
Vol. 2: Covers U.S. and Japanese carrier operations in the Pacific.

BRYAN, JOSEPH. *Aircraft Carrier*. New York: Ballantine Books, 1954.
A candid diary of Bryan's brief service aboard the USS *Yorktown* in early 1945.

BRYAN, JOSEPH, and REED, PHILIP. *Mission Beyond Darkness*. New York: Duell, Sloan and Pearce, 1945.
A detailed first-hand account of the attack on a Japanese fleet by Air Group 16 of the USS *Lexington* in the concluding phase of the Battle of the Philippine Sea on 19 June 1944.

BURNS, EUGENE. *Then There Was One: The U.S.S. Enterprise and the First Year of War*. New York: Harcourt, Brace, 1944.
Personal narrative of the operations of the USS *Enterprise* in the first year of the war.

CASEY, ROBERT J. *Torpedo Junction: With the Pacific Fleet from Pearl Harbor to Midway*. Indianapolis, New York: Bobbs-Merrill, 1942.
An exciting record of the first six months of the war, particularly the battle of Midway.

DATER, HENRY M., USNR. *Airfields at Sea: The Development of Carrier Warfare*. Hagerstown, Md.: Fairchild Engine & Airplane Corp., n.d.
A brief but insightful history of the aircraft carrier and its role in World War II.

DICKINSON, CLARENCE E., with SPARKS, BOYDEN. *The Flying Guns: Cockpit Record of a Naval Pilot from Pearl Harbor through Midway*. New York: Charles Scribner's Sons, 1942.
Dickinson provides an exciting account of his exploits in the first six months of the war.

FERRIER, H. H. "Torpedo Squadron Eight, the Other Chapter." *U.S. Naval Institute Proceedings* 90 (October 1964): 72–76.
A member of Torpedo Squadron Eight, Ferrier was part of a detachment of the squadron sent to defend Midway Island in June 1942. Thus he participated in the battle but not in the same way as his more famous squadron mates who flew off the *Hornet*.

FORGY, HOWELL M. *And Pass the Ammunition*. New York: Appleton-Century, 1944.
A Navy chaplain's account of Pearl Harbor and subsequent duty aboard a cruiser at the Coral Sea.

FRANK, PAT, and HARRINGTON, JOSEPH D. *Rendezvous at Midway: USS Yorktown and the Japanese Carrier Fleet*. New York: John Day, 1967.
The story of *Yorktown* and her role in the Battle of Midway.

173

FUCHIDA, MITSUO, and OKUMIYA, MASATAKE. *Midway—The Battle that Doomed Japan*. Annapolis: U.S. Naval Institute, 1955.
Two Japanese airmen, one a Zero pilot and the other an air power strategist, explain why the Japanese were defeated at Midway.

GLINES, CARROLL V. *Doolittle's Tokyo Raiders*. Princeton: D. Van Nostrand, 1964.
An almost day-by-day account of the famous Doolittle raid on Tokyo in April 1942.

HAGOROMO SOCIETY OF KAMIKAZE DIVINE THUNDERBOLT CORPS SURVIVORS. *The Cherry Blossom Squadrons: Born to Die*. Edited and supplemented by Andrew Adams. Translated by Nobuo Asahi and the Japan Tech Co. Los Angeles: Ohara Publications, 1973.
Originally published in Japanese in 1952, this book is a collection of memories, comments and criticisms of the Divine Thunderbolt Corps drawn from material submitted by survivors of the Kamikaze Corps and the members of the families of dead pilots.

HALSEY, WILLIAM F., and BRYAN, JOSEPH III. *Admiral Halsey's Story*. New York: McGraw-Hill, 1947.
Fleet Admiral Halsey gives his personal account of the combat operations in which he commanded.

HOYT, EDWIN P. *Blue Skies and Blood: The Battle of the Coral Sea*. New York: Paul S. Eriksson, 1975.
A lively and well-documented account of the Battle of the Coral Sea.

INOGUCHI, RIKIHEI, and NAKAJIMA TADASHI, with PINEAU, ROGER. *The Divine Wind: Japan's Kamikaze Force in World War II*. Annapolis: U.S. Naval Institute, 1958.
Both Japanese authors served with the Kamikaze Corps and have provided an intimate glimpse of the motivations of the kamikaze pilots and the suicidal flight operations.

ITO, MASANORI, with PINEAU, ROGER. *The End of the Imperial Japanese Navy*. Translated by Andrew Y. Kuroda. New York: W. W. Norton, 1962.
A detailed account of the history of the Japanese Navy in World War II from the point of view of a knowledgeable Japanese participant and observer.

JOHNSTON, STANLEY E. *The Grim Reapers*. New York: E. P. Dutton, 1943.
The story of Fighting Ten (VF 10) covering the Battles of the Coral Sea, Midway, Guadalcanal and Santa Cruz.

————. *Queen of the Flat-Tops: The U.S.S. Lexington and the Coral Sea Battle.* New York: E. P. Dutton, 1942.
The story of the USS *Lexington* in the Battle of the Coral Sea told by a participant.

KARIG, WALTER, HARRIS, RUSSELL L., and MANSON, FRANK A. *Battle Report: The End of an Empire,* 5 vols. New York: Holt, Rinehart and Winston, 1944–52.
A standard source for U.S. naval operations in World War II, the series draws on official records, battle reports, and personal narratives.
Vol. 1: Pearl Harbor and Coral Sea
Vol. 2: Atlantic
Vol. 3: Pacific—middle phase
Vol. 4: End of an Empire
Vol. 5: Victory in the Pacific

KING, ERNEST J. *U.S. Navy at War 1941–1945.* Official reports to the Secretary of the Navy by Fleet Admiral Ernest J. King, U.S. Navy, Commander in Chief, United States Fleet and Chief of Naval Operations. Washington: U.S. Navy Department, 1946.
The official version of U.S. naval operations.

LAWSON, TED W. *Thirty Seconds Over Tokyo.* Edited by Robert W. Considine. New York: Random House, 1943.
The story of one pilot and his crew in the Doolittle raid on Tokyo in April 1942.

LORD, WALTER. *Day of Infamy.* New York: Holt, Rinehart and Winston, 1957.
A classic account of the Japanese attack on Pearl Harbor.

————. *Incredible Victory.* New York: Harper & Row, 1967.
An exhaustively researched reconstruction of the Battle of Midway told by an able historian.

MILLOT, BERNARD. *Divine Thunder: The Life and Death of the Kamikazes.* Translated by Lowell Bair. New York: McCall, 1970, 1971.
A Frenchman's analysis of the origins and operations of all kinds of kamikazes.

MORISON, SAMUEL E. *History of United States Naval Operations in World War II.* 15 vols. Boston: Little, Brown, 1947–1962.
Volumes III–VIII, XII–XIV are the standard references on the war in the Pacific.

————. *The Two-Ocean War: A Short History of the United States Navy in the Second World War.* Boston: Little, Brown, 1963.

A one-volume condensation of Morison's multivolume history of the U.S. Navy in World War II.

OKUMIYA, MASATAKE, and HORIKOSHI, JIRO, with CAIDIN, MARTIN. *Zero!* 2d ed. New York: E. P. Dutton, 1959.
Two Japanese, an aviator and staff officer and an experienced aeronautical engineer, explain why the Zero fighter was so dominant in the first part of the war and also why American air power gradually came to dominate the war.

PAWLOWSKI, GARETH L. *Flat-Tops and Fledglings: History of American Aircraft Carriers.* South Brunswick, N.J.: A. S. Barnes, 1971.
A brief account of the history of each carrier that the U.S. Navy has ever had. Filled with facts and data. Illustrated.

POLMAR, NORMAN. *Aircraft Carriers: A Graphic History of Carrier Aviation and Its Influence on World Events.* London: Macdonald, 1969; Garden City, N.Y.: Doubleday, 1969.
An essential study of the development of the aircraft carrier. Profusely illustrated.

POTTER, EDWARD B., and NIMITZ, CHESTER W., eds. *Sea Power: A Naval History.* Englewood Cliffs, N.J.: Prentice-Hall, 1960.
A helpful supplement to Morison's history which covers all the major battles and has an extensive number of maps.

POTTER, JOHN DEANE. *Yamamoto: The Man Who Menaced America.* New York, Viking Press, 1965.
A biography of the Japanese commander in chief which helps to put him in the context of Japanese politics as well as naval operations.

REYNOLDS, CLARK G. *The Fast Carriers: The Forging of an Air Navy.* New York: McGraw-Hill, 1968.
An interpretive history of the development of the Fast Carrier Task Force in the U.S. Navy and Royal Navy in the Pacific in World War II. Covers carrier doctrine, policies and the personalities who formulated and/or carried out these policies.

SAKAI, SABURO, with CAIDIN, MARTIN, and SAITO, FRED. *Samurai!* New York: E. P. Dutton, 1958.
A Japanese fighter ace tells his story of the air war.

SHERMAN, FREDERICK C. *Combat Command: The American Aircraft Carriers in the Pacific War.* New York: E. P. Dutton, 1950.
A senior U.S. Navy carrier commander explains how the flattops helped bring victory to the United States.

SIMS, EDWARD H. *Greatest Fighter Missions of the Top Navy and Marine Aces of World War II.* New York: Harper & Row, 1962.
This book contains brief biographies of all the top Navy and Marine Corps aces.

SMITH, STAN E., ed. *The United States Navy in World War II.* New York: William Morrow, 1966.
A lengthy anthology of first-hand accounts of U.S. naval operations in the war.

STAFFORD, EDWARD E. *The Big E: The Story of the USS Enterprise.* New York: Random House, 1962.
A biography of the U.S. carrier which fought in more battles than any other from Pearl Harbor to Okinawa.

TAYLOR, THEODORE. *The Magnificent Mitscher.* New York: W. W. Norton, 1954.
An even-handed biography of one of the U.S. Navy's great aviators and carrier commanders.

THACH, JOHN S. "The Red Rain of Battle: The Story of Fighter Squadron 3." *Collier's* 110 (December 12, 1942): 16 ff.
The commanding officer of VF 3 tells what his squadron did at Midway.

TOLAND, JOHN, *But Not in Shame.* New York: Random House, 1961.
An exhaustive account of the first six months of the war in the Pacific.

———, *The Rising Sun: The Decline and Fall of the Japanese Empire 1936–1945.* 2 vols. New York: Random House, 1970.
The war in the Pacific based upon extensive research and interviews which gives depth and feeling to the Japanese point of view.

TULEJA, THADDEUS V. *Climax at Midway.* New York: W. W. Norton, 1960.
An indispensable account of the Battle of Midway.

U.S. DEPARTMENT OF DEFENSE, WEAPONS SYSTEMS EVALUATION GROUP, WSEG STAFF STUDY NO. 4. *Operational Experience of Fast Carrier Task Forces in World War II.* Washington: DOD, August 15, 1951.
A detailed quantitative and qualitative analysis of Fast Carrier Task Force operations in World War II.

U.S. NAVY, OFFICE OF THE CHIEF OF NAVAL OPERATIONS. *U.S. Naval Aviation in the Pacific: A Critical Review.* Washington: Government Printing Office, 1947.
A brief account of U.S. naval aviation operations in World War II which sums up the "lessons" learned about air and carrier operations during the war.

UNITED STATES STRATEGIC BOMBING SURVEY. *Campaigns of the Pacific War*. Washington: Government Printing Office, 1946.
An official source for all the Pacific campaigns which has detailed organizational charts, reliable statistics and maps of key battles. A valuable reference.

————. *Interrogations of Japanese Officials*. 2 vols. Washington: Government Printing Office, 1946.
Postwar interrogations of both important and minor Japanese naval officers which cover nearly every major battle. Some transcripts are brief, others are very extensive.

WINTON, JOHN, ed. *The War at Sea: The British Navy in World War II*. New York: William Morrow, 1967, 1968.
An anthology of personal accounts of the British Navy in World War II which has some materials on Royal Navy carrier operations.

WOODWARD, C. VANN. *The Battle for Leyte Gulf*. New York: Macmillan, 1947.
A fair treatment of Admiral Halsey within the context of the broader scope of all parts of the Battle of Leyte Gulf.

YOSHIDA, MITSURU. "The End of *Yamato*." *U.S. Naval Institute Proceedings* 58 (February 1952): 117–129.
A survivor of the *Yamato's* suicide run during the Battle of Okinawa tells his story of what happened on the last sortie of that superbattleship.

Index

181

182